Camp on Wheels

Your Passport to RV Camping in National Parks

David Clark

Table of Contents

INTRODUCTION **6**

CHAPTER I: The RV Lifestyle **8**

Exploring the RV lifestyle 8

Types of RVs and their pros and cons 10

Benefits of RV travel 12

CHAPTER II: Choosing the Right RV **16**

Factors to consider when selecting an RV 16

Budget considerations 19

New vs. used RVs 21

CHAPTER III: Preparing Your RV for the Road **24**

Essential RV equipment and accessories 24

Maintenance and safety checks 27

Packing tips for your RV adventure 29

CHAPTER IV: National Park Basics **33**

Introduction to national parks........................ 33

History and significance of national parks 35

Different types of national park units 38

CHAPTER V: Planning Your National Park Adventure **41**

Researching and selecting national parks to visit 41

Making campground reservations...................... 44

Seasonal considerations 47

CHAPTER VI: Navigating the National Park System......... 50

National Park Service programs and passes 50

Entrance fees and passes 52

Rules and regulations within national parks 54

CHAPTER VII: Campground Life 57

Types of campgrounds within national parks 57

Camping amenities and facilities 59

Tips for a comfortable and enjoyable stay 61

CHAPTER VIII: Exploring the Great Outdoors 64

Outdoor activities and recreational opportunities in
national parks 64

Hiking, biking, wildlife watching, and more 66

Safety guidelines for outdoor adventures 68

CHAPTER IX: Cooking and Dining on the Road 72

Tips for RV cooking and meal planning 72

Campfire cooking and recipes 74

Food storage and safety 76

CHAPTER X: Staying Connected on the Road 80

Communication options while RVing 80

Internet and mobile connectivity 82

Staying in touch with loved ones 84

CHAPTER XI: RVing with Pets 87

Traveling with pets in your RV 87

Pet-friendly national parks and campgrounds 89

Pet safety and etiquette 91

CHAPTER XII: RVing Etiquette and Conservation 94

RV campground etiquette 94

Leave No Trace principles 96

Supporting the preservation of national parks 99

CHAPTER XIII: RV Maintenance and Troubleshooting ... 102

Basic RV maintenance tasks 102

Common RV issues and how to address them 104

Emergency preparedness 106

CHAPTER XIV: Capturing the Memories 110

Photography and journaling tips 110

Preserving your RV travel memories 112

Sharing your experiences with others 114

CHAPTER XV: RVing Community and Resources 116

Connecting with other RVers 116

Online RV forums and communities 118

Recommended books, websites, and apps 120

CONCLUSION 123

INTRODUCTION

Welcome to "Camp on Wheels: Your Passport to RV Camping in National Parks." This book is your guide to embarking on an unforgettable journey into the heart of nature, combining the comforts of home with the freedom of the open road. Whether you're a seasoned RVer or a novice looking to discover the wonders of national parks, this comprehensive guide will be your trusted companion on this epic adventure.

The RV lifestyle has captured the imaginations of countless individuals and families seeking a unique and immersive way to explore the great outdoors. In "Camp on Wheels," we will delve into every aspect of RV travel, from choosing the perfect rig to navigating the intricacies of national park reservations.

National parks are a treasure trove of natural beauty, history, and culture, and RV camping allows you to experience them like never before. We'll guide you through planning your national park adventure, providing tips on where to go, what to do, and how to make the most of your visit.

Whether you're seeking the tranquility of a remote campground, the thrill of hiking scenic trails, or the joy of sharing campfire stories under a starlit sky, "Camp on Wheels" has you covered. Along the way, you'll learn about responsible camping, delicious campfire recipes, staying connected on the road, traveling with pets, and much more.

So, buckle up, prepare to hit the road, and let "Camp on Wheels" be your passport to RV camping in national parks. The adventure of a lifetime awaits you, and this book is your key to unlocking the wonders of the great outdoors while enjoying the comforts of your rolling home.

CHAPTER I

The RV Lifestyle

Exploring the RV lifestyle

The RV lifestyle is a captivating and liberating way of life that has captured the hearts of countless individuals and families worldwide. At its core, it represents the perfect union of adventure and comfort, allowing enthusiasts to embark on epic journeys while taking their homes with them on wheels. This lifestyle has transcended mere travel; it is a philosophy of embracing the open road, connecting with nature, and savoring the freedom of the journey.

One of the most defining aspects of the RV lifestyle is its sheer diversity of options. From modest campervans to luxurious motorhomes, an RV suits every taste and budget. This diversity ensures that anyone, from retirees seeking a leisurely exploration of the countryside to young families on a quest for adventure, can find an RV that aligns with their specific needs and desires. The ability to customize an RV to fit one's lifestyle is a hallmark of the RV community, allowing individuals to make their homes on wheels truly their own.

The allure of RVing goes far beyond the acquisition of a vehicle. It is a lifestyle that fosters a profound connection to the great outdoors. RV enthusiasts are driven by a desire to immerse themselves in the beauty of nature, and their vehicles become gateways to some of the most breathtaking landscapes on the planet. Whether it's waking up to the serene beauty of a lakeside campground, or witnessing the grandeur of a national park's towering peaks, RVers are intimately connected with the natural world.

One of the fundamental appeals of the RV lifestyle is the sense of freedom it provides. You're not tied to hotel reservations or flight schedules when traveling in an RV. Instead, you're the master of your own destiny, free to change your route on a whim, stay an extra day in a captivating location, or discover hidden gems that aren't on any tourist maps. The flexibility of the RV lifestyle allows travelers to embrace spontaneity and the unexpected, creating truly unique and unforgettable memories.

Another aspect that makes the RV lifestyle so special is its strong sense of community. RVers often form close-knit bonds with fellow enthusiasts they meet on the road. Campground gatherings, potluck dinners, and shared campfires create opportunities for socializing and forging connections with like-minded individuals from diverse backgrounds. These connections can lead to lifelong friendships, providing a sense of belonging that enriches the RV experience.

However, the RV lifestyle is not without its challenges. It requires adaptability and self-sufficiency, as RVers must learn to troubleshoot and address maintenance issues that can arise during their travels. Living in a confined space also necessitates efficient organization and a minimalist approach to possessions. But these challenges are often outweighed by the sense of adventure and the rewards of exploration.

Ultimately, the RV lifestyle represents a departure from the ordinary and an embrace of a life less constrained. It encourages a shift away from materialism, inviting individuals to focus on experiences and relationships over possessions. Downsizing and simplifying one's life to fit into an RV can be freeing, allowing people to prioritize what truly matters to them.

In conclusion, the RV lifestyle is a unique and enriching way of life that allows individuals and families to explore the world while maintaining the comforts of home. It fosters a deep connection to nature, a sense of freedom, and a strong sense of community. While it may come with challenges, the rewards of the RV lifestyle are immeasurable, offering a profound sense of adventure, discovery, and connection to the world around us. It is an invitation to leave the ordinary behind and embark on a lifetime journey, where the road becomes your canvas, and every mile is a brushstroke in the masterpiece of your RV adventure.

Types of RVs and their pros and cons

Recreational Vehicles (RVs) come in various shapes and sizes, each designed to cater to the unique needs and preferences of different travelers. Choosing the right RV can significantly impact the overall travel experience, and understanding the various types, along with their pros and cons, is essential for making an informed decision.

Motorhomes, the first category of RVs, offer the convenience of an all-in-one package. Class A motorhomes are often considered the luxury liners of the RV world, offering spacious interiors and a wide range of amenities. They provide a comfortable and luxurious travel experience, with features like full kitchens, multiple bedrooms, and ample storage space. However, their size can be a drawback, making them less maneuverable and challenging to park in some areas. Additionally, they tend to be the most expensive option in terms of purchase price and fuel consumption.

Class B motorhomes, on the other hand, are more compact and resemble large vans. Their small size makes them easy to drive and maneuver, and they can often fit into standard parking spaces. While they offer better fuel efficiency and are a more affordable option, their limited space means fewer amenities and less storage. Class B motorhomes are an excellent choice for solo travelers or couples looking for a nimble and economical option.

Class C motorhomes fall between Class A and Class B, offering a compromise between space and maneuverability. They typically have an overhead sleeping area and a variety of amenities, making them suitable for families or larger groups. However, like Class A motorhomes, they can be challenging to navigate in tight spaces and may have higher operating costs.

Travel trailers are another popular category of RVs, known for their versatility. They come in various sizes and floorplans, allowing travelers to choose the one that best suits their needs. The primary advantage of travel trailers is that they can be towed by a wide range of vehicles, from trucks to SUVs. This flexibility means travelers can unhook their RV and use their vehicle for exploration once they've set up camp. However, towing a travel trailer requires some skill and practice, and some people may find it intimidating.

Fifth-wheel trailers are a subset of travel trailers that attach to a pickup truck using a hitch mounted in the truck bed. This design provides stability and better maneuverability than traditional travel trailers, making them an attractive option for those who plan to spend extended periods on the road. Fifth-wheel trailers often feature spacious interiors and luxurious amenities, but they require a compatible tow vehicle, limiting the choices for some travelers.

Truck campers are compact RVs that sit in the bed of a pickup truck. They are an excellent option for those who want the convenience of an RV but prefer the ability to detach their vehicle for off-road exploration. Truck campers come in various sizes, offering different comfort levels and amenities. While they are compact and lightweight, they may not provide as much living space as larger RVs.

Popup campers, also known as tent trailers, are the smallest and most basic type of RV. They are lightweight and foldable, making them easy to tow and store. Popup campers are a budget-friendly option, but they lack the amenities and comfort of larger RVs. They are best suited for those who enjoy a more rustic camping experience and do not require extensive amenities.

In conclusion, the choice of an RV type depends on individual preferences, travel goals, and budget considerations. Class A motorhomes offer luxury but have a higher price tag and limited maneuverability. Class B motorhomes are compact and efficient but sacrifice space and amenities. Class C motorhomes strike a balance between the two. Travel trailers offer versatility and can be towed by various vehicles but may require towing experience. Fifth-wheel trailers provide stability and space but need a compatible tow vehicle. Truck campers are compact and offer off-road capability. Popup campers are budget-friendly but lack amenities. Ultimately, understanding the pros and cons of each type of RV is essential for selecting the one that will best enhance the travel experience, ensuring a comfortable and enjoyable journey on the open road.

Benefits of RV travel

Recreational Vehicle (RV) travel has surged in popularity recently, and for good reason. This unique mode of travel offers many benefits that appeal to a wide range of travelers, from adventure-seekers to those looking for a more relaxed and comfortable way to explore the world. Whether you're a seasoned RV enthusiast or considering embarking on your first RV journey, understanding the advantages of RV travel can help you appreciate the beauty of life on the open road.

One of the most significant benefits of RV travel is its unparalleled sense of freedom. When you travel in an RV, you are not bound by strict itineraries or fixed schedules. You can chart your own course, change plans on a whim, and linger in places that captivate your heart. RV travel allows you to escape the confines of traditional travel, where you must adhere to airline schedules or hotel check-out times. Instead, you can wake up to a stunning sunrise over a tranquil lakeside and decide to extend your stay, all while maintaining the comfort and familiarity of your own mobile home.

Another advantage of RV travel is immersing yourself in the natural world. RVers often seek out campgrounds in national parks, forests, or along scenic routes, offering them the chance to experience the beauty of nature up close. Whether it's waking up to the sound of birdsong, witnessing the majesty of a snow-capped mountain range, or falling asleep under a star-studded sky, RV travel provides a direct connection to the great outdoors that is unparalleled by traditional forms of travel. Nature becomes your neighbor, and the world becomes your backyard.

RV travel also promotes a more sustainable and eco-friendly way of exploring the world. Unlike air travel, which can have a significant carbon footprint, RVs are relatively fuel-efficient compared to the number of travelers they can accommodate. Additionally, RVers often adopt more sustainable practices, such as conserving water and reducing waste, as they are responsible for their own resources on the road. Many RVers embrace the "leave no trace" ethos, leaving the natural environment as pristine as they found it, and supporting the preservation of our planet's natural wonders.

One of the joys of RV travel is the opportunity to forge strong connections with fellow travelers. RV campgrounds and parks often foster a sense of community, with like-minded individuals sharing stories, experiences, and camaraderie. Campfire gatherings, potluck dinners, and impromptu social events are common occurrences, making it easy to meet new friends and create lasting memories with people from all walks of life. The RV community is known for its warmth and hospitality, and it's not uncommon for travelers to form lifelong friendships on the road.

RV travel also promotes a more relaxed and stress-free way of exploring. With your own kitchen and bathroom facilities onboard, you have the convenience of home wherever you go. You can cook your favorite meals, sleep in your own bed, and have all your essentials within arm's reach. No need to worry about checking in and out of hotels, packing and unpacking, or dining out for every meal. This level of comfort and convenience allows you to focus more on the experiences and adventures of your journey and less on travel logistics.

Furthermore, RV travel is an ideal option for families and multi-generational trips. It offers a way for family members to bond and create lasting memories while having the space and amenities they need. Parents can have quality time with their children, and grandparents can enjoy special moments with their grandchildren, all within the cozy confines of the RV. It's an opportunity for shared adventures and quality family time, fostering connections that can last a lifetime.

In conclusion, the benefits of RV travel are diverse and far-reaching. It offers a unique sense of freedom, a deep connection to nature, eco-friendly travel options, and the opportunity to build lasting friendships within the RV community. RV travel promotes a relaxed and comfortable way of exploring the world while fostering quality family time and creating unforgettable memories. Whether you're a seasoned RVer or considering your first trip, the allure of the open road and the advantages of RV travel await, promising a journey filled with adventure, discovery, and the freedom to explore on your own terms.

CHAPTER II

Choosing the Right RV

Factors to consider when selecting an RV

Choosing the right RV (Recreational Vehicle) is pivotal for anyone considering the RV lifestyle. The variety of available options can be overwhelming, and selecting the perfect RV for your needs involves carefully considering several factors. Each type of RV offers its own advantages and drawbacks, making it essential to assess your travel preferences, budget, and lifestyle before making a decision.

The first factor to consider is the type of RV that suits your needs. RVs come in various categories, including motorhomes, travel trailers, fifth-wheel trailers, truck campers, and pop-up campers. Each type has its unique characteristics and advantages. Motorhomes, for instance, provide a self-contained travel experience with amenities like a kitchen, bathroom, and sleeping quarters all in one vehicle. Travel trailers offer flexibility and can be towed by various vehicles, allowing you to separate your living space from your travel vehicle. Fifth-wheel trailers provide stability and space but require a compatible tow vehicle with a fifth-wheel hitch. Truck campers are compact and versatile, fitting in the bed of a pickup truck. Popup campers are budget-friendly and lightweight, offering a more rustic camping experience. Selecting the right type of RV depends on your travel preferences, your family or group size, and your budget.

Once you've determined the type of RV that suits your needs, you'll need to consider size and layout. RVs come in various lengths and floorplans; the layout can significantly impact your comfort and convenience. A smaller RV might suffice if you're traveling solo or with a partner, offering easier maneuverability and lower operating costs. Families or larger groups may require more space, and RVs with multiple bedrooms, bathrooms, and living areas may be necessary. It's essential to visualize your daily routines and determine the best layout to accommodate your lifestyle.

Budget is another critical factor in selecting an RV. The cost of RVs can vary widely, from affordable options like pop-up campers and some travel trailers to high-end motorhomes and fifth-wheel trailers. Beyond the initial purchase price, it's crucial to consider ongoing expenses such as maintenance, fuel, campground fees, and insurance. Establishing a budget that accounts for both the upfront cost and long-term expenses will help you make a more informed decision.

One often overlooked aspect of RV selection is the choice between new and used vehicles. New RVs offer the latest features, warranties, and the peace of mind that comes with a brand-new vehicle. However, they come with a higher price tag. On the other hand, used RVs are more budget-friendly but may require a thorough inspection to ensure they are in good condition. It's essential to weigh the benefits of a new RV against the potential savings of a used one, considering factors like depreciation and maintenance history.

Consider the features and amenities that are important to you in an RV. Modern RVs can come equipped with various conveniences, including full kitchens, bathrooms, entertainment systems, and climate control. Assess your priorities, whether it's a spacious kitchen for cooking gourmet meals on the road, a comfortable bedroom, or advanced technology for connectivity and entertainment.

Prioritizing your must-have features will help you narrow down your options.

Evaluating the tow vehicle or chassis is crucial if you're considering a towable RV like a travel trailer or fifth-wheel. Ensure that your existing vehicle or the one you plan to purchase can safely tow your desired RV. Consider factors such as towing capacity, hitch compatibility, and whether you need additional towing equipment like sway control or weight distribution hitches.

Another essential factor to consider is the storage and carrying capacity of the RV. Assess whether it provides adequate space for your belongings, outdoor equipment, and necessities. Consider whether it has storage compartments, and whether they are easily accessible. Insufficient storage can lead to a cramped and cluttered living space, detracting from your overall RV experience.

Lastly, don't forget to consider RV ownership's long-term aspects. Consider how the RV will fit into your lifestyle and travel plans over the years. Think about maintenance requirements, the availability of service and repairs, and the resale value of the RV. This long-term perspective will help ensure that your RV continues to meet your needs as your journey unfolds.

In conclusion, selecting the right RV involves carefully evaluating factors such as type, size, layout, budget, new or used status, features and amenities, tow vehicle compatibility, storage, and long-term considerations. Each factor is crucial in determining the RV that will best suit your lifestyle and travel goals. By conducting thorough research and assessing your preferences, you can make an informed decision that leads to a rewarding and enjoyable RV experience, whether you're embarking on weekend getaways or full-time RV living.

Budget considerations

Choosing the right RV (Recreational Vehicle) is about finding the ideal vehicle to match your travel preferences and ensuring that it aligns with your budget. RV ownership costs extend far beyond the initial purchase price, and prospective RVers must carefully consider their financial situation to make an informed decision. Budget considerations encompass various aspects, from the upfront cost of the RV to ongoing expenses like maintenance, insurance, fuel, and campground fees.

The initial purchase price is the first and most apparent budget consideration when selecting an RV. RVs come in a wide range of prices, from relatively affordable options like pop-up campers and some travel trailers to high-end motorhomes and fifth-wheel trailers that can cost hundreds of thousands of dollars. The RV's type, size, age, and brand all play a significant role in determining the price. It's crucial to establish a budget before starting the RV shopping process and stick to it to avoid overspending.

In addition to the upfront cost, buyers should also factor in taxes and registration fees associated with RV ownership. These expenses can vary by state and region, so it's essential to research the specific costs in your area. Depending on the purchase price and your state's tax rates, these additional fees can substantially add to your overall expenses.

Beyond the purchase price and associated fees, ongoing expenses are significant when budgeting for RV ownership. Fuel costs are a substantial part of RV travel, and the type and size of the RV can significantly impact fuel efficiency. Smaller, more aerodynamic RVs are more fuel-efficient, while larger motorhomes and trailers can be less economical. Travelers should estimate their expected mileage and fuel costs based on the RV they plan to purchase and the destinations they intend to visit.

Maintenance is another ongoing expense that cannot be overlooked. Regular maintenance is essential to keep the RV in safe and reliable condition. Maintenance tasks may include engine and chassis care, appliance and systems checks, roof and seal inspections, and tire maintenance. Budgeting for routine maintenance and occasional repairs is crucial to ensure the longevity of the RV and avoid unexpected financial burdens.

Insurance is another essential budget consideration for RV owners. The type and amount of insurance coverage needed can vary depending on the RV's value, intended use (full-time or occasional), and specific features. Comprehensive insurance coverage can provide protection in case of accidents, theft, vandalism, or damage from natural disasters. Shopping around for insurance quotes and choosing a policy that fits your budget while providing adequate coverage is advisable.

Campground fees are an ongoing expense for RV travelers, and the cost can vary widely depending on the campground type and location. RVers can choose from various camping options, from public campgrounds and national parks with lower fees to private RV resorts with higher nightly rates. Budget-conscious RVers can save money by choosing more affordable campgrounds and occasionally opting for boondocking or dry camping, which often costs less or nothing at all.

Another significant budget consideration is the cost of RV storage. When not in use, RVs require a place to be stored safely. Options for RV storage include renting a dedicated RV storage space, utilizing a storage facility, or finding a secure spot on your property if local regulations allow. Storage costs can vary based on location, RV size, and whether it is stored indoors or outdoors.

Travelers should also account for costs associated with RV accessories and equipment. RVs may require additional gear like hoses, leveling blocks, towing equipment, and kitchen supplies. These expenses may seem small individually but can add up, so budgeting for these necessities is essential.

Finally, creating a contingency fund in your budget is advisable for unexpected expenses or emergencies. Like any other vehicle, RVs can experience breakdowns or unforeseen issues that may require immediate attention and repair. Setting aside a financial cushion for such situations can provide peace of mind and prevent unexpected financial stress.

In conclusion, budget considerations are fundamental to selecting an RV that aligns with your financial situation and travel goals. Prospective RVers should establish a clear budget that covers the initial purchase price, taxes, registration fees, ongoing expenses like fuel, maintenance, insurance, campground fees, storage, accessories, and potential emergencies. By carefully assessing these financial aspects, RV owners can confidently embark on their adventures, knowing they have planned for the full range of expenses associated with RV ownership and travel.

New vs. used RVs

The decision to purchase an RV (Recreational Vehicle) is exciting, but it comes with a significant choice: whether to buy a new or a used RV. Each option has its own advantages and considerations, and making the right decision requires careful consideration and assessment of your preferences, budget, and travel plans.

Let's begin by examining the advantages of buying a new RV. A brand-new RV offers the latest features, technology, and amenities. You'll be the first to enjoy the vehicle's pristine condition, free from the wear and tear that comes with previous ownership. New RVs typically come with manufacturer warranties, providing peace of mind and financial protection in case of unexpected issues. With a new RV, you can select the specific model, floorplan, and options that best suit your needs and preferences. This level of customization can be appealing for those who want to create their dream RV from the ground up.

However, purchasing a new RV also comes with its own set of considerations, starting with the price. New RVs are generally more expensive than their used counterparts. The initial cost can be a significant investment, requiring a larger budget or financing. The depreciation of a new RV is another factor to keep in mind. RVs tend to depreciate in value rapidly during the first few years of ownership, which means that if you decide to sell or trade in your new RV, you may not recoup the full purchase price.

On the other hand, buying a used RV offers several compelling advantages, primarily related to cost savings. Used RVs are generally more budget-friendly, making it easier for individuals or families to enter the world of RV travel without a substantial upfront expense. Depreciation is less of a concern with used RVs since they have already experienced their steepest depreciation during the early years of ownership. This can be especially appealing for those who want to maximize their investment and potentially upgrade to a newer RV in the future without significant financial loss.

Used RVs also benefit from having any initial issues or manufacturing defects already addressed. If the previous owner encountered any problems or made upgrades or improvements, you may inherit these enhancements, saving you time and money. Additionally, used RVs often come with a history of maintenance and repair records, providing insight into how well the vehicle has been cared for and maintained.

However, there are some potential downsides to consider when purchasing a used RV. The availability of used RVs with specific features or floorplans may be limited, as you'll choose from what's currently on the market. Depending on the age and condition of the RV, you may need to invest in maintenance or upgrades to bring it up to your desired standard. It's essential to have a thorough inspection conducted before finalizing the purchase to identify any potential issues that may need immediate attention.

Choosing between a new or used RV ultimately depends on your budget, preferences, and priorities. If you value having the latest technology and features, are willing to pay a premium, and plan to keep the RV for an extended period, a new RV may be the right choice for you. On the other hand, if you're budget-conscious, don't mind a few miles on the odometer, and are comfortable with the idea of potentially making some upgrades, a used RV can offer a more cost-effective entry into the RV lifestyle.

In conclusion, the decision to buy a new or used RV is a significant one that should align with your financial situation and travel goals. New RVs offer the latest features and customization but have a higher price tag and faster depreciation. Used RVs provide cost savings and may have already addressed initial issues but may require some maintenance and have limited availability. Careful consideration of your budget and priorities will help you make the right choice and confidently embark on your RV adventure, whether you're exploring the open road in a brand-new vehicle or a well-loved, pre-owned RV.

CHAPTER III

Preparing Your RV for the Road

Essential RV equipment and accessories

Equipping your RV (Recreational Vehicle) with the right gear ensures a comfortable, safe, and enjoyable travel experience. While the specific equipment and accessories you need may vary depending on your RV type and travel style, there are several essential items that every RV owner should consider. These items enhance convenience, safety, and comfort, making your RV adventure all the more memorable.

One of the first considerations is leveling blocks and stabilizers. Keeping your RV level is crucial for the proper functioning of appliances and comfort while parked. Leveling blocks or leveling pads help you achieve a stable and level surface at your campsite. Stabilizers can reduce rocking and sway when you're inside your RV.

Managing wastewater is a crucial aspect of RV life, and to do this effectively, you'll need a high-quality sewer hose and connectors. Ensure you have the necessary fittings to connect to campground dump stations or sewer hookups. A clear sewer hose adapter can help monitor the flow of waste, making it easier to know when your tanks are empty.

Access to freshwater is equally important, and a dedicated freshwater hose for your RV is essential for connecting to campground water supplies. Consider a hose with a built-in filter to ensure clean and safe drinking water. Having a pressure regulator to protect your RV's plumbing from high water pressure is also a good idea.

Wheel chocks and X-Chocks play a crucial role in securing your RV in place when parked. Wheel chocks go under your tires, preventing your RV from rolling, while X-Chocks fit between tandem tires, reducing movement and sway.

An RV surge protector is another essential piece of equipment to safeguard your RV's electrical system from voltage spikes and surges that can cause damage. It helps protect your RV's electronics and appliances.

To navigate safely and efficiently, consider investing in an RV-specific GPS system. It can provide directions suitable for your RV's height, weight, and length and identify RV-friendly routes and points of interest.

A well-equipped tool kit is indispensable for minor RV repairs and maintenance tasks. Include essential tools like screwdrivers, pliers, wrenches, and a tire pressure gauge. Remember to have the necessary tools for maintaining your RV's specific systems.

Regular toilet paper can clog your RV's holding tanks, so it's essential to use RV-specific toilet paper designed to dissolve quickly and prevent blockages.

Safety should always be a priority, so ensure your RV has a working fire extinguisher and smoke detector. Regularly check and maintain these safety devices.

Accidents can happen, so having a well-stocked first aid kit is essential. Include bandages, antiseptic wipes, pain relievers, and any specific medications or supplies you may need.

Create a comfortable outdoor living space with camping chairs and an outdoor mat. It's an excellent way to relax and enjoy the fresh air while at your campsite.

Enhance the comfort of your RV's mattress with a quality mattress topper. It can significantly affect the quality of your sleep during your travels.

An awning or sunshade provides shade and protection from the sun, allowing you to enjoy the outdoors without getting too hot. It also helps keep the interior of your RV cooler.
Protecting your RV from the elements is crucial for its longevity. Invest in RV covers designed for your specific type and size of RV to shield it from sun, rain, and snow when not in use.
Vent covers allow you to keep your roof vents open even during inclement weather. They provide ventilation while preventing rain from entering your RV.

A sewer hose support system keeps your sewer hose off the ground, ensuring a consistent downhill flow for efficient drainage.

RVs require specialized cleaning products to maintain their finishes and surfaces. Invest in RV-approved cleaners for the interior and exterior of your vehicle.

Depending on your preferences, bring camping gear such as a portable grill, stove, cooking utensils, and outdoor tableware to enhance your culinary adventures while camping.
Lastly, consider bringing entertainment options like board games, books, DVDs, or portable electronic devices to keep everyone entertained during downtime or inclement weather.
While this list provides an overview of essential RV equipment and accessories, tailoring your gear to your specific travel plans and preferences is critical. Careful preparation and investment in quality equipment can make your RV adventures more comfortable, enjoyable,

and stress-free, ensuring that your time on the road is filled with unforgettable experiences and memories.

Maintenance and safety checks

Owning an RV (Recreational Vehicle) is a rewarding experience that provides the freedom to explore the open road and create lasting memories. However, with this freedom comes the responsibility of maintaining and ensuring the safety of your RV. Regular maintenance and safety checks are crucial to keeping your RV in optimal condition and ensuring your and your passengers' safety during your travels.

One of the most important aspects of RV maintenance is keeping up with routine inspections and service. Just like any vehicle, your RV requires regular maintenance to keep it running smoothly. This includes oil changes, air filter replacements, and checking the condition of belts and hoses. Regular service for your RV's engine and chassis is essential to prevent breakdowns on the road.

Equally important is the maintenance of your RV's house systems. These systems include the plumbing, electrical, heating, and cooling systems. Regularly inspecting and servicing these systems can prevent costly repairs and ensure a comfortable living environment. Check for leaks, test all electrical outlets and appliances, clean or replace air filters, and have the furnace and air conditioner serviced as needed.

Tire maintenance is critical for RV safety. Check your tire pressure before every trip, as underinflated tires can lead to poor handling and increased fuel consumption. Additionally, inspect the tread depth and overall condition of the tires regularly. It's essential to replace tires that show signs of wear or aging to prevent blowouts, which can be dangerous, especially on a large RV.

Another crucial safety aspect is checking the brakes and wheel bearings. Have the brakes inspected and serviced as your RV manufacturer or service professional recommends. According to the manufacturer's guidelines, wheel bearings should be inspected and repacked with grease. Well-maintained brakes and wheel bearings are essential for safe stopping and handling.

Properly functioning propane systems are vital for cooking, heating, and cooling within your RV. Inspect the propane system for leaks and have it serviced regularly by a certified technician. It's also essential to ensure that propane detectors and alarms are working correctly to alert you to any potential issues.

RVs have multiple safety features designed to protect you and your passengers. Regularly test and maintain smoke detectors, carbon monoxide detectors, and fire extinguishers. These devices can save lives in the event of an emergency. Ensure all safety equipment is in good working order and replace batteries as needed.

RVs have a unique feature known as the generator, which provides power when you're not connected to shore power. Regularly service and maintain the generator to ensure it runs smoothly and provides reliable power. Change the oil, replace filters, and inspect the fuel system to prevent generator-related issues during your travels.

Another aspect of RV safety is keeping your RV's weight within its specified limits. Overloading your RV can lead to poor handling, increased fuel consumption, and even accidents. Carefully weigh your RV, including all your belongings, to ensure you're not exceeding weight limits. Distribute weight evenly and follow manufacturer guidelines for proper loading.

Regularly inspect the roof and seals of your RV to prevent leaks and water damage. Any damage to the roof or seals should be repaired promptly to prevent more extensive issues down the road. Roof maintenance is especially critical for avoiding costly repairs and maintaining the structural integrity of your RV.

As part of your safety checks, ensure all emergency equipment and supplies are readily accessible and in good condition. This includes first aid kits, emergency road kits, flashlights, and communication devices. Being prepared for emergencies can significantly affect your safety on the road.

Lastly, keeping a detailed maintenance and service log is invaluable. Record all service and maintenance tasks, including dates and mileage. This log can help you keep track of when specific tasks are due and provide a record of your RV's maintenance history, which can be valuable when selling or trading in your RV.

In conclusion, maintenance and safety checks are fundamental aspects of RV ownership. Regular inspections and servicing of your RV's systems, including the engine, house systems, tires, brakes, propane, and generator, are essential to prevent breakdowns and ensure a safe and comfortable travel experience. Additionally, regularly checking safety equipment and adhering to weight limits and loading guidelines contributes to RV safety. By prioritizing maintenance and safety, you can enjoy the freedom of the open road with peace of mind, knowing that your RV is in top condition and your passengers are safe.

Packing tips for your RV adventure

Packing for an RV (Recreational Vehicle) adventure is a unique endeavor that requires a thoughtful and organized approach. The limited space inside an RV necessitates carefully considering what to bring and how to maximize every inch of storage. Whether you're a seasoned RVer or embarking on your first trip, these packing tips can help you make the most of your RV's storage capacity while ensuring you have all the essentials.

First and foremost, creating a detailed checklist is an essential step before packing. This checklist should include all the items you'll need for your trip, categorizing them into essentials, nice-to-haves, and optional items. Having a checklist not only ensures that you won't forget crucial items but also helps you prioritize what to bring and avoid overpacking with non-essentials.

One of the fundamental principles of RV packing is to limit non-essential items. RV space is at a premium, and every item you bring should serve a purpose or enhance your experience. Leave behind items you can live without, focusing on what you truly need for your journey. Remember that many supplies and replacements can often be found on the road if needed.

Thinking in terms of multi-functionality is a key strategy for efficient packing. Opt for items that can serve multiple purposes. For example, collapsible kitchenware and utensils save space and can be used for cooking and dining. A multi-tool or Swiss Army knife can handle various tasks, eliminating the need for a collection of single-purpose tools. Similarly, consider versatile clothing that can be layered for different weather conditions, reducing the number of outfits you must bring.

Meal planning is another essential aspect of RV packing. Plan your meals in advance and stock your RV with non-perishable foods that can serve as the foundation for multiple dishes. This approach saves space and simplifies your shopping and meal preparation during your journey. Be sure to account for any dietary restrictions or preferences to ensure you have the right ingredients on hand.

Consider using vacuum-sealed storage bags for bulky clothing items like jackets, blankets, and bedding to optimize storage space. These bags can significantly reduce the volume of these items, freeing up valuable storage space in your RV. The same principle applies to clothing – pack efficiently, and choose versatile pieces that can be mixed and matched for different occasions and weather conditions.

Organization is paramount in RV packing. Utilize clear, stackable storage bins to keep items well-organized and easily accessible. Label these bins to identify their contents, making it more straightforward to locate what you need. Group similar items together in bins to streamline the packing and unpacking process, further enhancing your overall RV experience.

Maximizing vertical space is another crucial strategy for efficient packing. Consider adding shelves or storage organizers inside closets and cabinets to maximize vertical storage opportunities. Hanging shoe organizers can be used for more than just shoes – they can hold toiletries, cleaning supplies, or other small items. You can make the most of your RV's storage capacity by utilizing vertical space effectively.

Safety should always be a priority when packing for an RV adventure. Ensure that essential safety items, such as first aid kits, fire extinguishers, and emergency tools, are readily accessible and in good condition. Regularly check and maintain these safety devices to ensure they are fully functional.

Lastly, don't forget to plan for outdoor gear if your RV adventure includes activities like camping, hiking, or biking. Consider how you'll transport and store these items on or in your RV, keeping in mind that they should be secure and easy to access when needed.

In conclusion, packing for an RV adventure is a balancing act between comfort and functionality. You can make the most of your RV's storage space by creating a detailed checklist, limiting non-essential items, thinking about multi-functionality, and planning meals wisely. Efficient organization, using space-saving solutions, and prioritizing safety all contribute to a successful and enjoyable RV adventure. Remember that RV packing is a skill that improves with experience, so embrace the process and fine-tune your approach to suit your travel style and preferences. Ultimately, the goal is to maximize the comfort and convenience of your journey while savoring the freedom and flexibility of RV travel.

CHAPTER IV

National Park Basics

Introduction to national parks

National parks are not merely protected areas of stunning natural beauty but windows into the soul of a nation's landscapes, history, and culture. These pristine expanses of wilderness and cultural heritage are preserved and maintained by governments to ensure that present and future generations can enjoy them. In this introduction to national parks, we will delve into the significance of these protected areas, explore their diverse ecosystems, and discuss their vital role in conservation, education, and recreation.

National parks are the jewels of a country's natural heritage, showcasing the grandeur and diversity of its landscapes. These protected areas can encompass many environments, from towering mountain ranges and dense forests to sprawling deserts and lush wetlands. Each national park is a unique microcosm of the natural world, offering a glimpse into the intricate web of life that thrives within its boundaries. Whether it's the otherworldly geothermal wonders of Yellowstone National Park, the dramatic cliffs of Yosemite, or the pristine beaches of Acadia, national parks capture the essence of a nation's natural beauty.

Beyond their aesthetic appeal, national parks hold profound historical and cultural significance. Many of these areas are rich in the heritage of indigenous peoples and the pioneers who explored and settled the land. Petroglyphs, ancient ruins, and historic buildings within these parks serve as a testament to the human history intertwined with the landscapes. Visitors can connect with the past, gaining a deeper understanding of the people and events that shaped the nation's history.

Conservation is a cornerstone of the mission of national parks. These protected areas are sanctuaries for countless species of flora and fauna, many of which are endangered or threatened. The preservation of these ecosystems ensures species' survival and maintains biodiversity, which is essential for the planet's health. National parks also serve as natural laboratories where scientists can research and gather data to understand better and address environmental challenges, such as climate change.

In addition to conservation, national parks play a vital role in education and public awareness. These protected areas provide opportunities for people of all ages to learn about the natural world, history, and cultural heritage. Interpretive programs, visitor centers, and ranger-led activities offer insights into each park's unique features and stories. Through these educational experiences, visitors gain a deeper appreciation for nature's value and conservation's importance.

Recreation is another fundamental aspect of national parks. Millions of visitors flock to these natural wonders each year to hike, camp, fish, paddle, and engage in various outdoor activities. National parks offer a chance to disconnect from the hustle and bustle of modern life and immerse oneself in the tranquility of the wilderness. Whether it's a challenging backcountry trek or a leisurely stroll along a scenic trail, national parks provide opportunities for adventure and rejuvenation.

It's important to note that national parks are not just isolated islands of protected land but part of a broader network of protected areas and conservation efforts. Many countries designate national parks as part of their commitment to preserving the environment and combating biodiversity loss. International organizations like the United Nations also recognize the importance of protected areas in achieving global conservation goals.

In conclusion, national parks are treasures that celebrate a country's natural beauty, cultural heritage, and ecological diversity. They serve as bastions of conservation, providing sanctuary for countless species and fostering scientific research. National parks also offer educational opportunities, fostering a deeper connection to the natural world and our shared history. Moreover, these protected areas provide recreational outlets for people seeking solace and adventure in the great outdoors. As we embark on this journey to explore national parks further, we will delve into the unique characteristics of some of the world's most iconic and cherished natural and cultural landscapes.

History and significance of national parks

The concept of national parks, as we know them today, emerged in the 19th century, driven by a growing appreciation for the natural world and a desire to protect it for future generations. The history of national parks is a testament to humanity's evolving relationship with the environment and the recognition of the importance of conservation. This section will explore the history and significance of national parks, shedding light on their development, purpose, and enduring importance.

The origins of national parks can be traced back to the United States in the mid-19th century. The catalyst for this movement was the breathtaking landscape of Yosemite Valley in California. It was there that the artist and conservationist George Catlin proposed the idea of preserving natural wonders for the enjoyment of the public and the protection of their intrinsic value. However, it was not until 1872 that President Ulysses S. Grant signed the Yellowstone National Park Protection Act into law, designating Yellowstone as the world's first national park. This historic action laid the foundation for creating a global protected area network.

Yellowstone's designation as a national park marked a significant turning point in environmental conservation. It signaled a departure from the prevailing view that natural resources were inexhaustible and that wilderness should be tamed and exploited for economic gain. Instead, it introduced the radical idea that some places should be preserved in their pristine state, free from commercial development and resource extraction. This visionary approach recognized that the intrinsic value of these landscapes extended beyond their utility for human exploitation.

The national park movement gained momentum in the United States during the late 19th and early 20th centuries. Iconic parks such as Yosemite, Grand Canyon, and Glacier followed in Yellowstone's footsteps. These protected areas were established not only for their natural beauty but also for their cultural and historical significance. Historic sites and monuments, including battlefields, forts, and the homes of famous individuals, were added to the national park system to preserve the nation's heritage.

Beyond the United States, the idea of national parks spread to other countries, establishing similar protected areas worldwide. Canada established its first national park, Banff, in 1885, followed by creating national parks in countries like Australia, New Zealand, and South Africa. The global community recognized the importance of preserving the environment and biodiversity for future generations, and this shared commitment culminated in the establishment of the International Union for Conservation of Nature (IUCN) in 1948.

The significance of national parks extends far beyond their role as pristine landscapes and repositories of cultural heritage. These protected areas serve a multitude of vital functions. First and foremost, they are sanctuaries for biodiversity. National parks protect diverse ecosystems, ensuring the survival of numerous plant and animal species. By preserving these habitats, they play a crucial role in conserving biodiversity and preventing species extinction.

Moreover, national parks provide opportunities for scientific research and environmental monitoring. Researchers study these ecosystems to understand ecological processes better, track climate change impacts, and develop strategies for conservation and restoration. The knowledge gained from national parks contributes to our understanding of the natural world and informs global conservation efforts.

Education is another cornerstone of national parks. These areas allow visitors to connect with nature, learn about local ecosystems, and gain insights into cultural heritage. Interpretive programs, visitor centers, and ranger-led activities provide opportunities for experiential learning. Through educational experiences, national parks foster a deeper environmental appreciation and encourage responsible stewardship.

National parks also have a significant economic impact. They attract millions of visitors annually, stimulating local economies and creating jobs in nearby communities. The tourism industry associated with national parks generates revenue that can be reinvested in park maintenance and conservation efforts. Additionally, national parks contribute to the well-being of nearby residents by providing recreational opportunities and enhancing their quality of life.

In conclusion, the history and significance of national parks are intertwined with the evolution of humanity's relationship with the environment. These protected areas have their roots in the 19th-century conservation movement and have since become global symbols of the importance of preserving nature and cultural heritage. National parks serve as sanctuaries for biodiversity, hubs of scientific research, centers of education, and drivers of economic prosperity. Their enduring importance lies in their ability to inspire and connect people with the natural world and to ensure the conservation of our planet's most precious treasures for generations to come.

Different types of national park units

National park units in the United States come in diverse forms, each serving a unique purpose in preserving the nation's natural and cultural heritage. While the term "national park" often conjures images of vast, pristine landscapes, the National Park Service oversees a wide array of protected areas that collectively tell the story of the country's rich history and breathtaking landscapes.

Among the most iconic and well-known are the national parks themselves. These are designated to protect and showcase the country's most extraordinary natural and cultural features. Think of Yellowstone's geothermal wonders or the Grand Canyon's awe-inspiring vistas. These parks often span vast expanses, boasting diverse ecosystems and iconic landmarks.

National monuments, on the other hand, are designated to protect specific natural, cultural, or historical features. They can vary significantly in size and popularity. The Statue of Liberty National Monument, symbolizing freedom and democracy, is recognized worldwide, while the Devil Tower National Monument in Wyoming is celebrated for its distinctive geological formation.

National historic sites focus on preserving and interpreting places of historical significance. These units may include the homes of famous individuals, battlefields, or locations tied to pivotal events in the nation's history. For instance, the Martin Luther King, Jr. National Historic Site encompasses Dr. King's childhood home and the Ebenezer Baptist Church, where he preached.

In contrast to national parks, national preserves often emphasize resource management alongside conservation. While their primary goal is to protect natural resources, they may permit certain recreational activities such as hunting and fishing. Big Cypress National Preserve in Florida is renowned for its diverse wildlife and wetland ecosystems.

National recreation areas serve as multipurpose units offering outdoor recreation and conservation opportunities. They often encompass large reservoirs or river systems and provide various activities such as boating, fishing, hiking, and camping. Lake Mead National Recreation Area, straddling Nevada and Arizona, offers lakes, canyons, and historic sites.

National seashores are designated to protect unique coastal environments while facilitating beach-related recreation. These areas often include sandy beaches, dunes, marshes, and maritime forests. Cape Cod National Seashore in Massachusetts is a prime example, noted for its scenic beauty and ecological diversity.

National scenic trails are long-distance hiking trails that traverse some of the country's most stunning and remote landscapes. They offer backpackers a unique opportunity to immerse themselves in nature. The Appalachian National Scenic Trail, stretching from Georgia to Maine, is one of the most renowned.

National wild and scenic rivers aim to protect free-flowing rivers and their surroundings. These rivers are cherished for their pristine beauty, recreational opportunities, and ecological importance. The Rogue River in Oregon, renowned for its rugged canyons and vibrant salmon runs, is a designated national wild and scenic river.

National battlefield parks commemorate significant battles and military history, allowing visitors to learn about pivotal moments in the nation's past. Gettysburg National Military Park in Pennsylvania preserves the site of one of the Civil War's most iconic battles.

Finally, national memorials honor individuals, events, or ideas that have profoundly impacted American history and culture. These sites often feature iconic monuments and are visited by millions. The Lincoln Memorial in Washington, D.C., stands as a prominent example, paying tribute to President Abraham Lincoln and his enduring contributions.

In conclusion, national park units in the United States encompass diverse protected areas, each with its own distinctive purpose and significance. These units collectively celebrate the nation's natural and cultural heritage, from vast national parks to historic sites, seashores, and scenic trails. They provide recreation, education, and conservation opportunities, ensuring that the nation's diverse landscapes and history are preserved and accessible for generations to come.

CHAPTER V

Planning Your National Park Adventure

Researching and selecting national parks to visit

Planning an RV (Recreational Vehicle) trip to explore the vast expanse of national parks in the United States is a dream for outdoor enthusiasts and adventurers. The sheer diversity of these protected areas, each with its unique natural beauty, cultural significance, and recreational opportunities, can be exciting and overwhelming when planning your journey. To ensure your RV adventure is a success and that you visit the national parks that resonate most with your interests and aspirations, thorough research and thoughtful selection are paramount.

Begin by introspecting and identifying your interests and priorities. Ask yourself what type of natural landscapes or historical sites captivate you the most. Are you drawn to the grandeur of iconic landscapes like the Grand Canyon or Yellowstone? Or do you prefer the tranquility of lesser-known parks that offer a more intimate and secluded experience? Consider the activities that resonate with you, whether it's hiking, wildlife watching, photography, or exploring historical sites. Knowing your interests will guide your selection process, helping you narrow your choices and create an itinerary tailored to your passions.

One of the primary resources for researching national parks is the official website of the National Park Service (NPS). Here, you'll find comprehensive and detailed information about each park, including its geographical location, size, key attractions, visitor centers, available activities, and more. The NPS website also provides valuable tools such as maps, brochures, and visitor guides that can be downloaded or ordered to aid in your research and planning.

Beyond official resources, numerous travel guides and websites are dedicated to national parks and RV travel. These resources often offer in-depth information, insider tips, and recommendations from seasoned RVers and park enthusiasts. Popular guidebooks such as "National Geographic's Guide to National Parks" and online platforms like "The Dyrt" provide valuable insights and reviews to help you make informed decisions.

Logistics play a pivotal role in planning your RV trip to national parks. Evaluate practical factors like the distance between parks, road conditions, and accessibility for your RV. Ensure your RV is equipped to handle the terrain and weather conditions you may encounter on your journey. Additionally, consider the availability of campgrounds, RV hookups, and the necessity of making reservations, especially during peak seasons when campsite availability may be limited.

Park operating hours and seasons can significantly impact your visit. While some national parks are open year-round, others have limited accessibility during the winter months. Research the operating schedule of each park to determine when it is most suitable for your trip, considering factors like weather conditions and seasonal attractions.

Budget considerations are crucial when selecting national parks for your RV adventure. Entrance fees, camping fees, and other expenses can vary widely from one park to another. Some parks offer annual passes, such as the America the Beautiful Pass, which can provide substantial cost savings if you plan to visit multiple parks within a year. Factoring these costs into your budget will help you plan your journey effectively.

As you delve into the selection process, prioritize the national parks that are on your must-see list. Iconic parks like Yosemite, Zion, or the Great Smoky Mountains are often high on travelers' itineraries, and for good reason. These parks offer breathtaking landscapes and iconic landmarks that have captured the imaginations of generations. However, don't overlook the charm of lesser-known parks that can provide a quieter and more intimate experience, away from the crowds.

Seasons also play a vital role in your selection. Each season brings its unique experiences to national parks. Spring brings vibrant wildflower blooms, while summer offers warm weather and extended daylight hours for exploration. Fall showcases stunning foliage, and winter provides a serene and less-crowded ambiance. Consider the activities and scenery you prefer when planning your visit and the type of experience you want to create.

Finally, as you finalize your selection of national parks for your RV adventure, you must plan your itinerary meticulously. Outline your travel route, specific travel dates, and the duration of your stay at each park. While having a well-structured itinerary is essential, it's equally crucial to remain flexible and open to unexpected detours or extended stays if you fall in love with a particular destination.

Before embarking on your RV adventure, check the official NPS website for any park alerts, advisories, or road closures. These updates can help you adjust your plans and ensure a smooth and safe journey.

In conclusion, researching and selecting national parks for your RV trip is an exhilarating process that allows you to tailor your journey to your interests and preferences. Thoroughly research each park, considering logistics, budget, and seasonal factors, and carefully plan your itinerary. By taking these steps, you can look forward to a memorable and enriching RV journey through the natural wonders and cultural treasures of the United States' national parks.

Making campground reservations

Planning a successful RV (Recreational Vehicle) trip involves many elements, and one of the most crucial is securing campground reservations. As the popularity of RV travel continues to surge, the demand for campsites in national and state parks, private campgrounds, and even remote boondocking locations has increased significantly. To ensure a smooth and enjoyable RV journey, it is essential to understand the process of making campground reservations, the various types of campgrounds available, and some valuable tips for securing the ideal spot.

Before diving into the reservation process, being familiar with the different types of campgrounds suitable for RVers is essential. These include public campgrounds, private campgrounds, and the option of boondocking or dry camping. Public campgrounds, often found in national parks, state parks, and national forests, vary in terms of amenities, from primary sites with no hookups to full-service campgrounds offering water, electricity, and sewer connections. On the other hand, private campgrounds are managed by independent owners or companies, and their facilities can range from resort-like amenities to more rustic settings. Boondocking involves camping without hookups and often occurs in remote locations, relying on an RV's self-contained systems like generators and freshwater tanks.

The first step to initiate the reservation process is researching campgrounds in your intended destination. This research can involve exploring campground websites, consulting travel guides, and seeking recommendations from fellow RVers on online forums and social media groups. These sources provide valuable information about campgrounds, including details about their amenities, user reviews, and availability during different seasons.

Once you've identified your preferred campgrounds, the next step is to determine the dates of your RV trip. Consider the length of your stay at each location and be flexible with your travel dates. This flexibility can be particularly advantageous when making reservations during peak seasons, as it increases the likelihood of securing your preferred dates.

With your travel dates in mind, visit the official websites of the campgrounds you intend to stay at or utilize online reservation platforms like Recreation.gov, ReserveAmerica, or private campground booking websites. These platforms allow you to check campsite availability by entering your desired dates and specifying the type of RV site you require, such as full hookups, electric-only, or tent sites.

Once you've identified available campsites that meet your criteria, proceed to make your reservation online. Provide the necessary information, including your contact details, RV specifications, and payment method. Before finalizing your reservation, reviewing all the details and confirming your selection is essential.

After your reservation is completed, you will receive a confirmation email or receipt. It is vital to retain this confirmation document as a printed copy or accessible on your mobile device. This document includes essential information, including the campsite number, check-in/check-out times, and the campground's cancellation policies.

There are several helpful tips to remember to maximize your chances of securing campground reservations for your RV trip. First, plan your RV journey well in advance. Campgrounds tend to fill up quickly, especially in popular destinations and during peak seasons. Some campgrounds even accept reservations up to a year ahead of time. Being proactive in your planning ensures that you have the best selection of campsites.

Flexibility with your travel dates can also be advantageous. Consider adjusting your itinerary to take advantage of availability. Midweek stays or traveling during off-peak seasons often offer better campground options and reduced reservation competition.

Before finalizing your reservation, familiarize yourself with the campground's cancellation policy. Life can be unpredictable, and understanding the terms for cancellations and potential refunds is essential if your plans change.

To increase your chances of securing reservations, periodically monitor campground availability, especially if you initially couldn't secure your desired dates. Campground availability can change due to cancellations or last-minute openings.

Consider joining membership programs or loyalty rewards offered by some campgrounds. These programs can provide discounts and priority booking, particularly if you plan to visit specific campgrounds frequently.

As you prepare for your RV trip, remember check-in and check-out times at campgrounds. Arriving within the designated hours ensures a smooth arrival process and avoids inconveniencing campground staff or other campers.

Additionally, when reserving a campsite, pay attention to any length restrictions that may apply to RVs. Ensure your

RV fits comfortably within the designated site and complies with size limitations.

Lastly, take advantage of online resources and read reviews from previous campers. Reviews offer valuable insights into the campground's facilities, cleanliness, ambiance, and overall camping experience. These firsthand accounts can help you decide when selecting campgrounds for your RV trip.

In conclusion, making campground reservations for your RV trip is critical to travel planning. Understanding the types of campgrounds available, the reservation process, and valuable tips for securing a spot will help ensure a stress-free and memorable RV adventure. Whether you prefer public campgrounds, private resorts, or the freedom of boondocking, careful planning ensures that you can park your RV and make the most of your time exploring the natural wonders and cultural treasures the country offers.

Seasonal considerations

Embarking on an RV trip is an exciting and adventurous way to explore the great outdoors and experience the freedom of the open road. However, before you hit the highway, it's crucial to consider the season in which you plan to travel. Seasonal variations can significantly impact your RV journey, influencing everything from weather and road conditions to campsite availability and the activities you can enjoy. In this section, we will explore the seasonal considerations for RV trips, outlining the pros and cons of each season to help you make an informed decision for your next adventure.

Spring is a popular season for RV travel as it brings with it milder temperatures and blooming landscapes. The beauty of spring lies in the rejuvenation of nature, with flowers in full bloom and trees displaying vibrant shades of green. This season is ideal for outdoor enthusiasts who want to go hiking, fishing, or simply enjoy the beauty of nature. However, preparing for unpredictable weather is essential, as spring can bring occasional rain showers and rapidly changing conditions. Be sure to pack accordingly with waterproof gear and clothing.

Summer is the peak season for RV travel, as families take advantage of the school break and warmer weather. The long, sunny days are perfect for exploring national parks, lounging by the beach, and enjoying outdoor activities. Campgrounds tend to be crowded during this time, so making reservations well in advance is essential. The downside of summer travel is the scorching heat in certain regions, which can make RVs uncomfortably warm. Ensure your RV is equipped with air conditioning and consider traveling to cooler destinations if you're not a fan of high temperatures.

Autumn is a fantastic season for RV trips, often considered the best-kept secret among seasoned travelers. As the leaves change colors and the air becomes crisp, the scenery transforms into a breathtaking red, orange, and gold tapestry. The weather is generally pleasant, making it an ideal time for hiking, biking, and exploring small towns. Moreover, campgrounds are less crowded, allowing for a more peaceful and enjoyable experience. Be prepared for cooler nights, so bring layers and warm bedding to stay comfortable.

While RV travel during winter may not be everyone's cup of tea, it can offer a unique and serene experience for those who enjoy the snow and solitude. Heading to destinations in the northern regions, such as ski resorts or national parks, can provide winter sports like skiing and snowboarding opportunities. However, winter travel requires careful planning and preparation. Your RV must be winterized to prevent freezing pipes, and you'll need appropriate cold-weather gear to stay warm and safe. Also, road conditions can be hazardous, so check weather and road reports before going on a winter RV trip.

In conclusion, the season in which you choose to embark on an RV trip significantly impacts your overall experience. Each season has its advantages and challenges, and the choice ultimately depends on your preferences and interests. Whether you opt for the vibrant colors of fall, the warmth of summer, the freshness of spring, or the tranquility of winter, careful planning and preparation will ensure a successful and enjoyable RV adventure. So, consider the seasonal factors that matter most to you, and get ready to hit the road in your RV to create lasting memories and unforgettable experiences.

CHAPTER VI

Navigating the National Park System

National Park Service programs and passes

Embarking on an RV trip is a fantastic way to explore the natural beauty and cultural heritage of the United States. The National Park Service (NPS) is vital in preserving and maintaining some of the country's most iconic and pristine landscapes. To enhance the experience of RV travelers, the NPS offers various programs and passes that provide access to its parks and sites, making it easier and more affordable to enjoy the wonders of nature and history. This section will delve into the NPS programs and passes available for RV trips, highlighting their benefits and how they can enrich your travel experience.

The America the Beautiful Pass, often called the Annual Pass, is a valuable tool for RV enthusiasts. This pass grants access to over 2,000 federal recreation sites, including national parks, forests, wildlife refuges, and more for a reasonable fee. It covers the entrance fees for the pass holder and accompanying passengers in a single, private, non-commercial vehicle. The Annual Pass is ideal for RV travelers who plan to visit multiple parks and sites within a year, as it can significantly reduce the overall cost of admission.

In addition to the Annual Pass, the NPS offers specialized passes tailored to specific groups of RV travelers. The Senior Pass, available to U.S. citizens and permanent residents aged 62 and older, provides lifetime access to NPS sites at a nominal one-time fee. This pass is an excellent option for retirees looking to explore the beauty of America's natural landscapes during their RV journeys.

For RV travelers with disabilities, the Access Pass offers free lifetime access to NPS sites and discounts on specific amenities and services. This pass ensures that individuals with disabilities can fully enjoy the national parks and recreational areas, making their RV trips more inclusive and accessible.

Furthermore, the NPS collaborates with the U.S. military to provide the Annual Pass for active-duty military personnel and their dependents at no cost. This gesture acknowledges and honors the service of military members and their families, allowing them to enjoy the therapeutic benefits of nature during RV adventures.

Beyond passes, the NPS offers a range of programs and initiatives that enhance the RV trip experience. Junior Ranger programs engage young travelers by providing educational activities and opportunities to learn about the parks' environment, history, and culture. These programs can make RV trips more meaningful for families, fostering a deeper appreciation for the natural world.

RV travelers interested in cultural heritage and history will find the NPS Passport program intriguing. This program encourages visitors to collect cancellation stamps at various park visitor centers, creating a unique and personalized record of their journey through the NPS sites. It's a fantastic way to document your RV adventures and learn more about the significance of each park.

Additionally, the NPS offers interpretive programs, guided tours, and ranger-led activities in many parks. These programs provide valuable insights into the park's natural wonders and historical significance, enriching the RV trip with educational and immersive experiences.

In conclusion, the National Park Service programs and passes are invaluable resources for RV travelers seeking to explore the diverse and captivating landscapes of the United States. Whether you're an avid RV enthusiast, a retiree looking for adventure, a person with disabilities, a member of the military, or a family with young explorers, there are programs and passes tailored to enhance your RV journey. These offerings make the experience more affordable and provide opportunities for education, engagement, and appreciation of the nation's natural beauty and cultural heritage. So, as you plan your next RV adventure, be sure to consider the NPS programs and passes that can make your journey even more memorable and enjoyable.

Entrance fees and passes

Exploring the vast and stunning landscapes of the United States' national parks is a dream come true for many RV enthusiasts. However, it's essential to understand the entrance fees and pass options when planning an RV trip to these natural wonders. The National Park Service (NPS) manages a diverse range of parks, each with its own fee structure and pass options. This section will delve into entrance fees and passes in national parks for RV trips, providing valuable information to help travelers make informed decisions about their visits.

National parks vary in size, popularity, and amenities, which can influence the cost of entrance fees. The fees are typically used to fund park maintenance, conservation efforts, visitor services, and infrastructure improvements. For RV travelers, entrance fees are usually based on the vehicle size and the number of passengers. It's essential to check the specific entrance fees for the parks you plan to visit, as they can range from as low as $10 to as high as $35 or more per vehicle.

To make the experience more affordable and convenient, the National Park Service offers a range of passes that can significantly reduce the cost of entrance fees. The most popular of these passes is the America the Beautiful Pass, also known as the Annual Pass. This pass provides access to over 2,000 federal recreation sites, including national parks, forests, wildlife refuges, and more, for an entire year. It covers the entrance fees for the pass holder and all passengers in a single, private, non-commercial vehicle. The Annual Pass is a cost-effective option for RV travelers planning to explore multiple national parks during their journey.

The Senior Pass is a fantastic deal for RV travelers aged 62 and older. It offers lifetime access to national parks and other federal recreation sites at a one-time fee, making it a worthwhile investment for retirees looking to enjoy the country's natural beauty. Additionally, individuals with disabilities can obtain the Access Pass, providing free lifetime access to NPS sites and discounts on specific amenities and services, ensuring that these places remain inclusive and accessible to all.

The NPS also collaborates with the U.S. military to provide the Annual Pass for active-duty military personnel and their dependents at no cost. This gesture recognizes and honors the service of military members and their families, allowing them to experience the healing power of nature during RV adventures.

For travelers who plan to visit specific national parks repeatedly or those who are passionate about documenting their journeys, the NPS Passport program is a compelling option. This program encourages visitors to collect cancellation stamps at various park visitor centers, creating a unique and personalized record of their travels through the NPS sites. It adds a memorable and educational element to the RV trip experience.

In conclusion, entrance fees and passes in national parks are crucial in facilitating RV trips and ensuring that these remarkable natural treasures remain accessible to the public. RV travelers should take the time to research and plan accordingly, considering the specific fees and passes for the parks they intend to visit. The America the Beautiful Pass, Senior Pass, Access Pass, and Military Pass are excellent options for making these journeys more affordable and enjoyable. Furthermore, the Passport program adds a fun and educational dimension to the RV adventure. By understanding and taking advantage of these options, RV travelers can embark on unforgettable journeys through the United States' national parks, appreciating the beauty and wonder of these protected landscapes while supporting their conservation and preservation efforts.

Rules and regulations within national parks

Embarking on an RV trip to explore national parks' natural wonders and beauty is an exciting adventure. However, RV travelers must know and adhere to the rules and regulations established within these protected areas. National parks are designated to preserve the environment, wildlife, and cultural heritage, and following the rules ensures the conservation of these valuable resources while maintaining a safe and enjoyable experience for all visitors. In this section, we will delve into the essential rules and regulations within national parks that RV travelers should know when planning their trips.

One of the primary rules in national parks is the prohibition of littering. RV travelers must correctly dispose of their trash in designated receptacles to prevent environmental and wildlife harm. It's essential to pack out everything you bring into the park, leaving no trace of your visit.

Camping regulations vary from park to park, so you must familiarize yourself with the specific rules of the park you plan to visit. In many national parks, RV camping is allowed only in designated campgrounds, and reservations are often required, especially during peak seasons. Campfires may also be restricted, and you must adhere to any fire bans or guidelines set by the park service.

Wildlife viewing is a highlight of national park visits, but it's imperative to maintain a safe distance from animals. Feeding wildlife is strictly prohibited, as it disrupts their natural behaviors and can be harmful to their health. Approaching or feeding wildlife can also pose a significant danger to humans, as wild animals can be unpredictable. Off-road driving is generally not permitted in national parks, including driving an RV off designated roads or trails. RV travelers should stay on established roads and pull-offs to protect fragile ecosystems and prevent soil erosion.

It's essential to respect the park's natural and cultural features. Picking plants, removing rocks, or defacing natural formations is strictly prohibited. Similarly, removing or disturbing cultural artifacts, such as archaeological sites or historic structures, is illegal and can result in severe penalties.

Noise regulations are enforced to maintain visitors' peaceful and enjoyable experience. Excessive noise from generators or loud music can disturb the park's tranquility and the wildlife that calls it home. Quiet hours are typically established in campgrounds, and generators may be restricted during certain times.

In some national parks, pets are allowed, but they must be kept on a leash at all times and are often limited to specific areas. It's crucial to check the park's pet regulations and ensure you clean up after them to maintain a clean and safe environment.

Park rangers and staff are responsible for enforcing these rules and regulations, and violators may face fines, eviction from the park, or other legal consequences. RV travelers need to be aware of and respect these rules to ensure a positive experience for themselves and future generations of park visitors.

Lastly, Leave No Trace principles are valuable guidelines for RV travelers within national parks. These principles emphasize minimizing your environmental impact by disposing of waste properly, staying on designated paths, and respecting wildlife and other visitors. By adhering to these principles and following the rules and regulations set by the National Park Service, RV travelers can enjoy the beauty and serenity of national parks while contributing to their preservation for years to come.

CHAPTER VII

Campground Life

Types of campgrounds within national parks

National parks in the United States offer a diverse range of camping experiences, and RV travelers can find a variety of campgrounds to suit their preferences and needs. These campgrounds vary in terms of amenities, location, and level of accessibility, providing options for those who seek a rustic and secluded experience and those who prefer more modern conveniences.

Frontcountry campgrounds are the most common type of campgrounds within national parks. They are typically accessible by paved roads and are equipped with various amenities, including designated RV sites with hookups for electricity, water, and sewage. These campgrounds often have restrooms, showers, and picnic tables, making them suitable for RV travelers who prefer comfort and convenience. Reservations are recommended, especially during peak seasons, as frontcountry campgrounds tend to be popular and can fill up quickly.

Some national parks offer backcountry campgrounds for RV travelers seeking a more remote and rugged camping experience. These campgrounds are often accessible via unpaved roads or hiking trails and are situated in more secluded natural settings. RVs may not be able to access all backcountry campgrounds, so it's essential to check with the park's regulations and inquire about vehicle size restrictions. Backcountry campgrounds usually have fewer amenities and may not offer hookups, so RV travelers should be prepared for a more self-sufficient experience.

Primitive campgrounds are a step above backcountry camping but still offer a rustic experience. They are often situated in scenic locations within the park and provide basic amenities such as pit toilets and fire rings. While some primitive campgrounds may accommodate RVs, they typically do not have hookups, and RV travelers should be prepared to dry camp without access to electricity or sewage facilities. These campgrounds are an excellent choice for those who want a balance between seclusion and some essential amenities.

Group campgrounds are designed to accommodate larger parties, making them suitable for RV travelers on group outings or family reunions. These campgrounds offer shared facilities, including picnic areas, fire rings, and restrooms. Group campgrounds often require reservations and may have specific rules and restrictions regarding the number of people and vehicles allowed per site. They can provide a sense of community while still allowing for a camping experience within the park's natural beauty.

Some national parks have concession-operated campgrounds managed by private companies. These campgrounds typically offer a range of amenities, including RV hookups, showers, laundry facilities, and even on-site stores. While they may be more expensive than park-operated campgrounds, concession-operated campgrounds often provide more comfort and convenience for RV travelers. Making reservations in advance is advisable, as these campgrounds can also be in high demand.

In certain national parks, campgrounds may be open only during specific seasons due to weather conditions or maintenance schedules. RV travelers should check the park's official website or contact park rangers for information on seasonal campground availability. Planning your trip around the campground's operational season is essential to ensure a smooth and enjoyable RV experience.

In conclusion, national parks offer a diverse array of campgrounds, each catering to different preferences and needs of RV travelers. Whether you seek a frontcountry campground with full hookups and amenities or are adventurous enough to explore backcountry and primitive campgrounds, a camping option within national parks will suit your style. Before embarking on your RV trip, research the specific campgrounds available in the park you plan to visit, make reservations if necessary, and prepare accordingly to make the most of your national park camping experience.

Camping amenities and facilities

Camping has long been a beloved pastime for those seeking a break from the hustle and bustle of city life, and RV (Recreational Vehicle) trips have gained immense popularity among outdoor enthusiasts. RVs offer a unique way to experience the great outdoors while enjoying the comforts of home. One key factor contributing to the appeal of RV trips is the availability of a wide range of camping amenities and facilities. These amenities make RV camping a comfortable and enjoyable experience, allowing travelers to immerse themselves in nature without sacrificing convenience.

First and foremost, RV campgrounds are equipped with electrical hookups, water connections, and sewage disposal facilities. These essential amenities ensure that travelers can easily power their RVs, access clean water for cooking and bathing, and dispose of waste in an environmentally responsible manner. Electric hookups are particularly crucial, as they allow RVers to run appliances, charge devices, and enjoy air conditioning or heating systems, depending on the weather. With these amenities in place, RVers can enjoy the comforts of home while surrounded by the beauty of nature.

In addition to the essential utilities, many RV campgrounds provide amenities such as Wi-Fi and cable television hookups. This allows travelers to stay connected with the outside world and stay entertained during their downtime. While camping is often associated with disconnecting from technology, staying connected can be valuable for emergencies, work-related tasks, or simply keeping in touch with loved ones.

Another significant advantage of RV camping is the presence of well-maintained restroom and shower facilities. Unlike traditional camping, where campers might have to rely on portable toilets or dig their own latrines, RV campgrounds offer clean and modern restroom facilities. Access to showers with hot water is especially appreciated after a day of outdoor activities. These facilities enhance the overall camping experience, making it more accessible and enjoyable for individuals and families.

Many RV campgrounds have picnic tables, fire pits, and barbecue grills for those who enjoy cooking and dining outdoors. These amenities encourage campers to enjoy cooking over an open flame, sharing stories around a campfire, and savoring meals under the stars. Additionally, some campgrounds even offer on-site convenience stores or dining options, making it easy to stock up on supplies or enjoy a meal without the need to leave the campground.

Recreational activities are an integral part of RV camping, and many campgrounds provide a range of options to keep travelers entertained. These facilities cater to various interests and age groups, from hiking trails and fishing ponds to swimming pools and playgrounds. RV campgrounds often organize group activities and events, fostering a sense of community among campers.

Safety and security are paramount, and most RV campgrounds have on-site staff to assist campers and ensure their well-being. This can provide peace of mind for travelers, especially those new to RV camping or unfamiliar with the area. Additionally, well-lit campgrounds and designated areas for RVs contribute to a safe and secure environment for everyone.

In conclusion, camping amenities and facilities are vital in enhancing the RV camping experience. These amenities allow travelers to enjoy the beauty of the outdoors while still having access to essential comforts and conveniences. Whether it's electrical hookups, modern restrooms, recreational activities, or the opportunity to connect with others, RV campgrounds offer a wide range of amenities that cater to the needs and preferences of every camper. RV camping perfectly balances nature and comfort, making it an increasingly popular choice for outdoor enthusiasts seeking unforgettable adventures on the road.

Tips for a comfortable and enjoyable stay

Embarking on an RV (Recreational Vehicle) trip is an exciting adventure that allows you to explore new destinations while enjoying the comforts of home on wheels. Whether you're a seasoned RVer or a novice, there are several essential tips to ensure a comfortable and enjoyable stay during your RV trip.

First and foremost, thorough trip planning is critical. Research the destinations you intend to visit, including campgrounds and RV parks along your route. Make reservations in advance, especially during peak travel seasons, to secure a spot at your desired campground. This planning step will help avoid the stress of finding last-minute accommodations and ensure you have a place to park your RV.

Packing efficiently is crucial when traveling in an RV. While you have more space compared to traditional camping, it's still essential to prioritize items that are essential for your trip. Bring clothing suitable for various weather conditions, cooking utensils, and food supplies. Overpacking can lead to a cluttered and uncomfortable living space in your RV, so pack smartly and only bring what you truly need.

Maintenance checks are a must before hitting the road. Ensure your RV is in excellent working condition by inspecting the engine, tires, brakes, and all mechanical systems. Also, check the propane, water, and sewage systems to prevent unexpected issues during your trip. Regular maintenance will help you avoid breakdowns and make for a smoother journey.

When driving your RV, take your time and drive cautiously. RVs are larger and heavier than regular vehicles, requiring extra attention and care. Maintain a safe following distance, reduce your speed, and be mindful of the height and width of your RV when navigating through tunnels, bridges, and narrow roads. Familiarize yourself with the RV's handling characteristics to ensure a safer and more enjoyable driving experience.

Campground etiquette is essential to create a positive atmosphere for all campers. Be considerate of your neighbors by keeping noise levels down, especially during quiet hours. Dispose of trash in designated bins and follow campground rules regarding campfires and pet policies. Maintaining good campground etiquette ensures a peaceful stay and fosters a sense of community among fellow RV enthusiasts.

Conservation is a crucial principle of RV travel. Be mindful of your water and energy consumption to prolong your

RV's self-sufficiency. Use LED lights, turn off appliances when not in use, and conserve water during showers and dishwashing. Additionally, practice Leave No Trace principles when exploring the outdoors by respecting nature and leaving your campsite as pristine as you found it.

Safety should always be a priority during an RV trip. Equip your RV with necessary safety equipment, including fire extinguishers, smoke detectors, and a first-aid kit. Familiarize yourself with the location of emergency exits and safety procedures specific to your RV model. Be prepared for unexpected situations by having a communication plan in place and carrying a charged cell phone with you.

Finally, embrace the journey and savor the experience.

RV travel allows for connecting with nature, exploring new landscapes, and creating lasting memories with loved ones. Take time to relax and enjoy the unique comforts of RV living, such as cooking meals in your kitchen and stargazing from the comfort of your RV bed. Be flexible with your itinerary and allow room for spontaneous adventures along the way.

In conclusion, a comfortable and enjoyable RV trip requires careful planning, efficient packing, regular maintenance, safe driving, campground etiquette, conservation efforts, safety precautions, and a willingness to savor the journey. By following these tips and embracing the RV lifestyle, you can make the most of your RV adventure and create cherished memories that will last a lifetime. RV travel is not just a means of transportation; it's a way to experience the world with all the comforts of home.

CHAPTER VIII

Exploring the Great Outdoors

Outdoor activities and recreational opportunities in national parks

National parks hold a special place in the hearts of nature enthusiasts, offering breathtaking landscapes and a wide array of outdoor activities and recreational opportunities for visitors. These protected areas, often characterized by their stunning natural beauty and diverse ecosystems, provide a unique playground for adventurers of all ages. From hiking and camping to wildlife watching and photography, national parks offer abundant experiences that allow individuals to connect with the natural world.

Hiking is one of the most popular and accessible outdoor activities in national parks. Trails of varying lengths and difficulty levels cater to both novice and experienced hikers. Whether it's a short nature walk to admire wildflowers or a challenging trek to summit a mountain, national parks provide diverse hiking experiences. Hikers can explore canyons, traverse forests, and follow winding paths that lead to breathtaking vistas, all while immersing themselves in the sights and sounds of nature.

Camping is another beloved activity that allows visitors to immerse themselves fully in the beauty of national parks. Many parks offer campgrounds with well-maintained facilities, including designated campsites, fire rings, and restroom facilities. Camping beneath the stars, surrounded by the serenity of the wilderness, is an experience that fosters a deep connection with the natural world. Whether it's car camping, backcountry camping, or RV camping, national parks cater to various camping preferences.

Wildlife watching is a favorite pastime for those seeking encounters with the park's indigenous animals. National parks are home to many wildlife species, from large mammals like bears and elk to birdlife, reptiles, and amphibians. Visitors can observe these creatures in their natural habitats and learn about the importance of wildlife conservation. Many parks also offer ranger-led programs and guided tours that provide valuable insights into the park's unique ecosystems and the animals that call them home.

Photography enthusiasts find national parks to be a treasure trove of scenic beauty. Capturing the majesty of towering waterfalls, pristine lakes, colorful sunsets, and intricate geological formations can be a photographer's dream. The ever-changing play of light and shadow in national parks offers endless opportunities for creative and awe-inspiring shots. Photography allows visitors to document their experiences and share the natural wonders of national parks with others.

For those seeking more adventurous activities, national parks offer rock climbing, kayaking, and whitewater rafting opportunities. Climbers can test their skills on challenging rock faces, while paddlers can navigate rivers and lakes with stunning landscapes. These activities provide an adrenaline rush, allowing participants to connect with the environment more deeply.

Stargazing is a magical experience in national parks, where the absence of city lights allows for precise and unobstructed night sky views. Many parks have earned designations as International Dark Sky Parks, emphasizing their commitment to preserving the purity of the night sky. Astronomy programs and star parties are often held to educate visitors about the cosmos and provide a chance to observe celestial wonders through telescopes.

In conclusion, national parks offer many outdoor activities and recreational opportunities for individuals and families to enjoy. Whether it's hiking through pristine wilderness, camping under the stars, watching wildlife in its natural habitat, capturing stunning photographs, engaging in adventurous pursuits, or simply gazing up at the night sky, national parks provide a diverse range of experiences that allow people to connect with the natural world and create lasting memories. These protected areas are vital for preserving biodiversity and fostering a love of nature and a sense of stewardship for the environment. National parks genuinely offer something for everyone, making them a cherished resource for future generations.

Hiking, biking, wildlife watching, and more

National parks are sanctuaries of natural beauty and biodiversity, offering various outdoor activities for visitors to enjoy. Among the many recreational opportunities available, hiking, biking, wildlife watching, and other adventures are some of the most captivating ways to explore these protected areas.

Hiking in national parks is a timeless and cherished activity that allows visitors to immerse themselves in the natural world. With trails ranging from easy strolls to challenging backcountry routes, there is a hiking experience suitable for individuals of all ages and fitness levels. Hikers can traverse dense forests, ascend majestic peaks, wander through serene meadows, or follow trails along pristine rivers and lakes. Along the way, they can marvel at the diverse flora and fauna that call these parks home. The sensation of stepping away from the daily grind and into the heart of nature is a rejuvenating experience that hiking in national parks offers.

Biking enthusiasts find national parks to be ideal destinations for exploring the great outdoors on two wheels. Many parks offer dedicated bike paths and trails that wind through breathtaking landscapes. Whether it's a leisurely ride through a serene forest, an exhilarating descent down a mountain trail, or a scenic route along the coastline, biking in national parks provides an opportunity to connect with nature while enjoying physical activity. Cyclists can also explore park roads and scenic byways, taking in the natural beauty and stopping to appreciate vistas and points of interest along the way.

Wildlife watching is a favorite pastime for those eager to glimpse the fascinating creatures that inhabit national parks. These protected areas are havens for diverse wildlife, including iconic species such as bears, elk, bison, and eagles. Visitors can engage in a game of patience and observation, waiting quietly at vantage points to catch a glimpse of these majestic animals in their natural habitats. Additionally, many national parks offer ranger-led programs and guided tours that provide valuable insights into the park's unique ecosystems, wildlife behaviors, and the importance of conservation efforts.

Photography in national parks is a rewarding and creative pursuit, allowing visitors to capture the stunning landscapes, unique geological formations, and vibrant flora and fauna. The ever-changing play of light and shadow in these natural settings provides endless opportunities for photographers to capture the perfect shot. Photographs serve as mementos of unforgettable experiences and as a means of sharing the beauty of national parks with others, inspiring appreciation and conservation of these natural treasures.

For those seeking more adventurous experiences, national parks offer rock climbing, kayaking, whitewater rafting, and more opportunities. Rock climbers can test their skills on rugged cliffs, while paddlers can navigate through rivers and lakes surrounded by breathtaking scenery. These exhilarating activities provide an adrenaline rush, allowing participants to forge a deeper connection with the environment and push their limits.

Stargazing is a magical experience in national parks, especially in areas designated as International Dark Sky Parks. The absence of urban light pollution allows for clear and unobstructed night sky views, where the stars and celestial bodies shine brightly. Astronomy programs and star parties are often held to educate visitors about the cosmos and provide a chance to observe planets, galaxies, and other celestial wonders through telescopes.

In conclusion, national parks offer many outdoor activities and recreational opportunities that cater to diverse interests and preferences. Whether it's hiking through pristine wilderness, biking along scenic routes, observing wildlife in its natural habitat, capturing stunning photographs, engaging in adventurous pursuits, or stargazing under the clear night sky, national parks provide a rich tapestry of experiences that connect people with the wonders of the natural world. These protected areas are not only vital for conserving biodiversity but also for fostering a love of nature and a sense of stewardship for the environment. National parks truly offer something for everyone, making them cherished destinations for nature enthusiasts and adventurers alike.

Safety guidelines for outdoor adventures

National parks are renowned for their pristine natural beauty and the opportunity they offer visitors to engage in various outdoor activities. However, while these protected areas are ideal for exploration and adventure, it's essential to prioritize safety to ensure a memorable and risk-free experience. Whether you're hiking, camping, wildlife watching, or partaking in other outdoor adventures, adhering to safety guidelines is crucial to protect yourself, others, and the environment.

First and foremost, always plan ahead. Before embarking on any outdoor adventure in a national park, research the park's rules and regulations, trail conditions, weather forecasts, and potential hazards. Knowing what to expect and being prepared will help you make informed decisions and minimize risks. Additionally, inform someone of your plans, such as a friend or family member, and share your itinerary, expected return time, and emergency contact information. This precautionary measure ensures that someone knows your whereabouts and can alert authorities if necessary.

Proper equipment and clothing are essential for safety in national parks. Ensure that you have appropriate gear for your chosen activity and that it is in good condition. Hikers should have sturdy footwear, suitable clothing, navigation tools, and essentials like first-aid kits, headlamps, and ample water and food supplies. Camping gear should be well-maintained and appropriate for the conditions. Additionally, dress in layers to accommodate changes in weather and temperature, and always carry rain gear.

Stay on designated trails and paths to minimize the environmental impact and reduce the risk of getting lost. National parks have established these routes to protect fragile ecosystems and ensure visitor safety. Venturing off-trail can damage vegetation and disturb wildlife habitats, while also increasing the likelihood of accidents. Stick to established paths and respect trail closures for your safety and the preservation of the park.

Be aware of your surroundings at all times. Pay attention to trail markers, signage, and landmarks to prevent getting lost. Familiarize yourself with the park's geography, including the location of emergency exits, ranger stations, and water sources. If you're hiking in a group, stay together, and communicate regularly. Keep an eye on changing weather conditions, as sudden storms or temperature drops can pose significant risks.

Wildlife encounters are a typical highlight in national parks, but it's essential to maintain a safe distance and never approach or feed wild animals. Wild animals can be unpredictable, and getting too close can provoke defensive behaviors that may lead to injury. Always observe wildlife from a distance using binoculars or telephoto lenses and follow park guidelines for wildlife viewing. Additionally, store food securely to avoid attracting animals to your campsite, as human food can harm wildlife and create potentially dangerous situations. Practice Leave No Trace principles to minimize your impact on the environment. Pack out all trash, litter, and waste, and dispose of it in designated bins or carry it out with you. Avoid picking plants, disturbing wildlife, or defacing natural features. Respect the natural and cultural heritage of the park by following all rules and regulations. In an emergency, stay calm and use your preparedness and communication tools. If you become lost, stay put and signal for help using a whistle, mirror, or other signaling device. Call emergency services and provide your location and situation if you have cell phone reception. Remember that cell phone reception may be limited in remote areas, so always have alternative means of communication, such as a satellite phone or personal locator beacon.

In conclusion, safety is paramount when enjoying outdoor adventures in national parks. By planning ahead, having the right equipment, staying on designated trails, being aware of your surroundings, respecting wildlife and the environment, and knowing how to respond in emergencies, you can have a safe and enjoyable experience while preserving the natural beauty of these treasured places. Following safety guidelines protects you and ensures that future generations can continue to explore and appreciate the wonders of national parks.

CHAPTER IX

Cooking and Dining on the Road

Tips for RV cooking and meal planning

RV (Recreational Vehicle) travel offers a unique way to explore the great outdoors while enjoying the comforts of home. One essential aspect of RV life is cooking and meal planning, which can be both a rewarding and cost-effective way to enhance your RV experience. Here are some valuable tips to help you make the most of your RV kitchen and create delicious meals on the road.

Before hitting the road, take the time to plan your meals. Consider the duration of your trip, the number of people in your group, and the available storage space in your RV kitchen. Create a menu that includes a balance of easy-to-cook meals and more elaborate dishes, and make a shopping list to ensure you have all the necessary ingredients.

Stock your RV kitchen with essential pantry items such as non-perishable goods, spices, and condiments. Opt for versatile ingredients that can be used in multiple recipes. Canned goods, pasta, rice, and grains are excellent choices. Be mindful of limited storage space and avoid over-packing.

Simplify your cooking process by focusing on one-pot or one-pan meals. These recipes require fewer dishes and less cleanup. Consider dishes like stir-fries, pasta with sauce, or skillet meals that combine protein, vegetables, and grains in a single pot or pan.

Save time and effort by doing meal prep before you hit the road. Chop vegetables, marinate meat, and pre-assemble ingredients whenever possible. Vacuum-sealed bags can help preserve freshness and make storage more efficient.

In an RV kitchen, space is precious. Invest in collapsible or stackable cookware to maximize storage efficiency. Look for space-saving pots, pans, and utensils designed for RV use. Non-stick cookware is also a wise choice for easier cleanup.

Take advantage of outdoor cooking options like campfires, grills, or portable stoves. Outdoor cooking can add a fun and adventurous element to your RV experience while reducing the heat and odors inside the RV. Just be sure to follow fire safety guidelines and check the rules at your campsite.

Consider using cooking gadgets like slow cookers (crockpots), instant pots, or toaster ovens. These appliances can make cooking more convenient and versatile, allowing you to prepare a broader range of dishes with minimal effort.

Be mindful of food waste by using leftovers creatively in the next meal. For example, roast extra vegetables for dinner and use them in omelets or sandwiches the next day. Plan meals to use up perishable items before they go bad.

One of the joys of RV travel is exploring different regions and their culinary offerings. Visit local markets, farms, and specialty stores to discover unique ingredients and flavors. Incorporating local products into your meals can add a delightful twist to your RV cooking experience.

While it's fun to experiment with gourmet recipes, don't forget to savor simple pleasures like grilled cheese sandwiches, hot dogs, or s'mores over a campfire. These easy-to-make comfort foods can be some of the most memorable meals during your RV journey.

Keeping your RV kitchen clean is essential for food safety and a pleasant cooking environment. Clean up promptly after each meal, wash dishes, and wipe down surfaces. Regularly empty and clean the refrigerator to prevent odors and mold.

In conclusion, RV cooking and meal planning can be an enjoyable and rewarding part of your travel experience. You can create delicious meals while on the road by planning ahead, stocking up smartly, simplifying your cooking methods, prepping in advance, and making the most of your kitchen space. Whether you're whipping up a gourmet dinner or enjoying a simple campfire meal, the key is to embrace the freedom and flexibility that RV cooking offers and relish the adventure of culinary exploration during your RV journey.

Campfire cooking and recipes

Campfire cooking is one of the most iconic and cherished aspects of RV (Recreational Vehicle) travel. The aroma of crackling wood and the flickering flames of a campfire create a sense of nostalgia and camaraderie that is deeply ingrained in the RV lifestyle. Campfire cooking adds a rustic charm to your RV trip and allows you to savor delicious, outdoor-inspired meals. Here, we'll explore the art of campfire cooking and share some mouthwatering recipes that will elevate your RV journey.

Campfire cooking may seem like a simple endeavor, but it requires some preparation and technique. First, it's essential to have the right equipment, including a sturdy grate or grill grate that can be placed over the campfire. Campfire cooking can be done over an open flame, on a grill, or using a Dutch oven. Having a set of long-handled tongs, a spatula, and a cast iron skillet can also be very useful.

One of the classic campfire cooking methods is roasting. Whether it's marshmallows for s'mores or hot dogs on a stick, roasting is a fun and straightforward way to prepare food over the fire. Skewers or long sticks are perfect for roasting sausages, marshmallows, or even vegetables. Simply hold the food over the flames, turning it occasionally until it reaches your desired level of doneness.

Grilling is another popular campfire cooking technique. Place a grate over the campfire or use a portable campfire grill, and you're ready to grill everything from burgers and chicken to corn on the cob and kebabs. The campfire's smoky flavor enhanced the taste of the grilled food, making it a favorite among campers.

Dutch oven cooking is a fantastic option for those looking to take campfire cooking to the next level. Dutch ovens are versatile cast iron pots with lids that can be used to bake, roast, simmer, and fry various dishes. You can make everything from stews and casseroles to bread and desserts in a Dutch oven. They are a must-have for any serious campfire chef.

Now, let's explore some campfire recipes that will tantalize your taste buds during your RV trip:

Campfire Skillet Breakfast: Start your day with a hearty breakfast. In a cast iron skillet, cook bacon until crispy. Remove the bacon and set it aside. In the same skillet, sauté diced potatoes, bell peppers, and onions until they are tender. Add the cooked bacon back into the skillet and crack eggs on top. Cover with a lid and cook until the eggs are done to your liking. Garnish with cheese and fresh herbs for extra flavor.

Campfire Chili: Prepare a delicious chili by browning ground beef or turkey in a Dutch oven over the campfire. Add chopped onions, bell peppers, garlic, and canned diced tomatoes. Season with chili powder, cumin, and paprika. Stir in kidney beans and let it simmer until the flavors meld together. Serve with grated cheese and a dollop of sour cream.

Campfire Pizza: Satisfy your pizza cravings with this campfire twist. Spread pizza dough on a greased cast iron skillet or a campfire-safe pizza stone. Top it with tomato sauce, shredded mozzarella cheese, and your favorite toppings. Place the skillet over the campfire or on a grill grate and cook until the crust is golden and the cheese is bubbly.

Campfire Apple Cobbler: Make a campfire apple cobbler for a sweet treat. In a Dutch oven, combine sliced apples, sugar, and cinnamon. In a separate bowl, mix biscuit dough (prepared ahead of time) and drop spoonfuls on top of the apples. Cover the Dutch oven and place it over the campfire coals. Cook until the apples are tender and the biscuit topping is golden brown.

In conclusion, campfire cooking adds a delightful dimension to RV travel, allowing you to savor meals infused with the smoky, outdoor flavors of the campfire. Whether you're roasting marshmallows, grilling burgers, or preparing a gourmet Dutch oven meal, campfire cooking creates unforgettable memories and enhances the overall RV experience. So, gather around the fire, cook up some delicious recipes, and relish the joys of campfire cuisine on your next RV trip.

Food storage and safety

Ensuring food storage and safety is paramount when embarking on an RV (Recreational Vehicle) trip. Properly storing and handling food during your journey helps you maintain a safe and enjoyable dining experience and prevents foodborne illnesses that can put a damper on your adventure. Here, we'll explore essential tips and practices to follow for food storage and safety during your RV trip.

Before hitting the road, make food safety a top priority. This includes both the food you bring with you and the ingredients you purchase along the way. Start with clean, sanitized kitchen utensils, cookware, and surfaces inside your RV. Wash your hands thoroughly before handling food, and use cutting boards and utensils designated for specific food types to prevent cross-contamination.

Maintaining proper refrigeration is crucial to prevent the growth of harmful bacteria in perishable items. Ensure your RV's refrigerator operates at the correct temperature (below 40°F or 4°C). Use a refrigerator thermometer to monitor the temperature regularly. When loading the refrigerator, store raw meats, dairy products, and other perishables on the bottom shelves to prevent potential leakage onto other foods.

If your RV refrigerator has limited space, or if you need extra cold storage for beverages and perishables, consider using a cooler with ice packs. Pre-chill the cooler and use it to store items like vegetables, fruits, and drinks, reducing the load on your RV refrigerator.

When packing food for your RV trip, use airtight containers or resealable bags to prevent cross-contamination and keep food fresh. Consider portioning out ingredients in advance to minimize the handling of raw items. Label containers with dates to help keep track of freshness.

Check the expiration dates of packaged and canned foods before bringing them on your RV trip. Dispose of any items that have passed their expiration dates or show signs of spoilage, such as bulging cans or off-putting odors.

If you plan to cook frozen items during your RV trip, avoid thawing them at room temperature. Use the RV refrigerator for slow and safe thawing, or employ the cold water method by placing the sealed item in a waterproof bag and submerging it in cold water, changing the water every 30 minutes.

When cooking meals in your RV kitchen, ensure that food reaches the proper internal temperature to kill harmful bacteria. Use a food thermometer to verify the temperature, especially when preparing meats, poultry, and seafood. Safe minimum internal temperatures vary by type of food.

Try to prepare and consume food in amounts that won't leave you with excessive leftovers. If you do have leftovers, refrigerate them promptly and consume them within a reasonable timeframe, typically within three to four days.

Maintain good personal hygiene when handling food. Wash your hands frequently, especially after handling raw meat, poultry, or seafood. Use soap and warm water, scrubbing for at least 20 seconds. If water is scarce, use hand sanitizer with at least 60% alcohol.

The quality of water used for food preparation and washing dishes is crucial. Ensure your water is safe for consumption or use bottled water when in doubt. Avoid using water from unknown or unverified sources.

In conclusion, food storage and safety are vital aspects of a successful and enjoyable RV trip. By prioritizing food safety, maintaining proper refrigeration, practicing safe cooking techniques, and adhering to good hygiene practices, you can minimize the risk of foodborne illnesses and ensure that your meals are a source of delight rather than concern during your RV journey. A little attention to food safety goes a long way in making your RV trip safe and satisfying.

CHAPTER X

Staying Connected on the Road

Communication options while RVing

Recreational Vehicle (RV) travel has gained immense popularity in recent years as people seek the freedom to explore the great outdoors while still enjoying the comforts of home. Whether you're a full-time RVer or just taking a road trip, staying connected with the outside world is crucial. Fortunately, various communication options are available to RV enthusiasts, ensuring that they can keep in touch, access information, and even work remotely while on the road.

One of the most common communication options for RVers is cellular communication. With the widespread coverage of cellular networks across the United States and in many other countries, RVers can rely on their smartphones for voice calls, text messages, and internet access. Many RV parks and campgrounds offer good cellular reception, allowing travelers to stay connected even in remote locations. Some RVers invest in cell signal boosters or antennas to enhance connectivity, which can significantly improve reception in areas with weak signals.

In addition to cellular communication, satellite communication is viable for RVers who venture into more remote areas. Satellite phones and satellite internet services provide connectivity even in places where cellular signals are non-existent. This option is especially beneficial for those who need reliable internet access for work or staying connected with family and friends.

However, satellite communication can be expensive and may require specialized equipment.

For RVers who want to access the internet more cost-effectively, public Wi-Fi networks are widely available in many RV parks, campgrounds, and public areas. These networks allow travelers to connect their devices to the internet for free or for a small fee. However, the quality and security of public Wi-Fi networks can vary, so it's essential to exercise caution and use a Virtual Private Network (VPN) to protect sensitive information while using these networks.

Two-way radios, also known as walkie-talkies, are another communication option popular among RVers, especially when traveling with a group or exploring vast landscapes. These devices provide instant communication within a specific range, allowing RVers to stay in touch with fellow travelers without relying on cellular networks. Two-way radios are relatively inexpensive and easy to use, making them a practical choice for group communication during RV adventures.

For those who want to stay informed about weather conditions and emergencies while RVing, a weather radio can be a valuable addition to their communication arsenal. Weather radios provide real-time weather alerts and updates, helping RVers make informed decisions to stay safe during their travels. Many weather radios are battery-powered or have a hand-crank feature, ensuring they work even when electricity is unavailable.

In conclusion, communication options while RVing are diverse and adaptable to travelers' needs and preferences. Whether you rely on cellular networks for everyday communication, invest in satellite communication for remote adventures, or use a combination of methods, staying connected and informed is essential when exploring the open road in an RV. With the right communication tools and strategies, RV enthusiasts can make the most of their journey while ensuring their safety and peace of mind along the way.

Internet and mobile connectivity

In the age of constant connectivity, staying online while RVing has become a priority for many travelers. Whether you're a full-time RVer or just embarking on a road trip adventure, accessing the internet and maintaining mobile connectivity is crucial. Fortunately, there are various options and strategies to ensure you remain connected while exploring the great outdoors in your recreational vehicle (RV).

One of the most common methods of accessing the internet and mobile connectivity while RVing is through cellular networks. These networks have expanded their coverage significantly in recent years, making it possible to stay connected in many remote areas. RVers can rely on their smartphones, tablets, or dedicated mobile hotspots to access the internet, make voice calls, send text messages, and stay connected with family and friends. Many RV parks and campgrounds offer decent cellular reception, allowing travelers to maintain their digital presence even in remote locations.

Some RVers invest in cellular signal boosters or antennas to maximize mobile connectivity. These devices can significantly enhance signal strength and improve reception in areas with weak signals. By installing an external antenna and connecting it to a signal booster, RVers can enjoy more reliable internet access and better call quality, ensuring they can work remotely or stream their favorite content without interruptions.

Satellite internet is a viable option for those who frequently venture into areas with limited or no cellular coverage. Satellite internet services offer nationwide coverage, making it possible to stay online in even the country's most remote corners. Although satellite internet can be more expensive than cellular plans, it provides a reliable and consistent internet connection. RVers interested in satellite internet will need to install a satellite dish on their RV, and subscription fees may vary depending on data usage and the provider.

Public Wi-Fi networks are another option for RVers seeking internet connectivity. Many RV parks, campgrounds, coffee shops, libraries, and public spaces offer free or low-cost Wi-Fi access. These networks are convenient for checking emails, browsing the web, and performing basic online tasks. However, the quality and security of public Wi-Fi networks can vary widely, and they may not be suitable for activities that require a secure and stable connection, such as remote work or online gaming.

RVers should consider using a Virtual Private Network (VPN) to enhance security and privacy when using public Wi-Fi networks. A VPN encrypts internet traffic, making it more difficult for hackers to intercept sensitive information. It also allows users to access geo-restricted content and maintain their privacy while browsing the web.

In conclusion, internet and mobile connectivity have become essential aspects of RV travel, enabling travelers to work remotely, stay in touch with loved ones, and access information on the go. Whether you rely on cellular networks, invest in satellite internet, or take advantage of public Wi-Fi networks, multiple options suit your connectivity needs while RVing. By understanding the available options and considering your travel destinations, you can ensure that you remain connected and enjoy a seamless online experience while exploring the open road in your RV.

Staying in touch with loved ones

Recreational Vehicle (RV) travel offers the allure of adventure, freedom, and exploration of the great outdoors. However, while RVing provides the opportunity to disconnect from the daily grind, staying connected with loved ones is also essential. Whether you're a full-time RVer or embarking on a temporary road trip, maintaining those vital connections with family and friends is crucial for emotional well-being and peace of mind.

One of the simplest and most common ways to stay in touch with loved ones while RVing is through modern technology, primarily smartphones. The widespread coverage of cellular networks across the United States and many other countries allows RVers to use their smartphones for voice calls, text messages, and video chats. Services like FaceTime, WhatsApp, Skype, and Zoom make it easy to have face-to-face conversations, bridging the gap created by physical distance. These applications also allow you to share the breathtaking scenery and memorable moments of your RV journey, making loved ones feel more connected to your adventures.

To maximize communication with loved ones while on the road, consider investing in a reliable mobile hotspot or Wi-Fi router. These devices use cellular data to create a secure Wi-Fi network within your RV, enabling multiple devices to connect to the internet simultaneously. With a mobile hotspot, you can easily maintain online communication, browse social media, or even work remotely from virtually anywhere your RV takes you. This ensures you can stay in touch even in areas with limited or no public Wi-Fi access.

For those who prefer a more personal touch, traditional methods of communication still have their place. Sending postcards, handwritten letters, or care packages from your RV adventures can be a thoughtful and nostalgic way to connect with loved ones. Many RVers enjoy visiting local post offices or finding unique mailboxes along their routes to send these physical tokens of affection. The anticipation of receiving a handwritten letter or a surprise package can create excitement and strengthen bonds with loved ones back home.

Social media platforms provide another avenue to share your RVing experiences with friends and family. Platforms like Facebook, Instagram, and Twitter allow you to post real-time updates, photos, and videos of your journey. Sharing your adventures through social media keeps your loved ones informed and provides a way for them to engage with your experiences by liking, commenting, and sharing your posts. It's a fun and interactive way to maintain connections while on the road.

Another essential consideration is emergency communication. While RVing is generally a safe and enjoyable activity, unforeseen circumstances can arise. It's crucial to establish an emergency communication plan with loved ones. Ensure that they have access to your travel itinerary, contact information for nearby RV parks or campgrounds, and a way to reach you in case of an emergency. Sharing your location through smartphone apps like Find My iPhone or Google Maps can provide you and your loved ones an added layer of security and peace of mind.

In conclusion, staying in touch with loved ones while RVing is possible and essential for maintaining strong relationships and emotional well-being on the road. Modern technology, mobile hotspots, and social media platforms make it easier than ever to communicate and share your RV adventures in real-time. However, don't overlook the charm of traditional methods like handwritten letters and postcards, as they can add a personal touch to your connections. By staying connected and having an emergency communication plan in place, you can enjoy the freedom and adventure of RV travel while keeping your loved ones close, no matter how far from home you roam.

CHAPTER XI

RVing with Pets

Traveling with pets in your RV

For many RV enthusiasts, hitting the open road with their beloved furry companions is a dream come true. Traveling with pets in your recreational vehicle (RV) adds an extra layer of companionship and allows you to share unforgettable adventures. However, ensuring a safe, comfortable, and enjoyable journey for both you and your pets requires careful planning and consideration.

First and foremost, before setting out on your RV adventure with pets, make sure to prioritize their safety. This includes securing them in an appropriate restraint system while the RV is in motion. Various options are available, such as pet seat belts, harnesses, and pet carriers. These safety measures will prevent accidents and protect your pets in case of sudden stops or collisions.

Moreover, ensuring that your pets are up-to-date on vaccinations and have proper identification is essential. Keep their medical records, tags, and microchip information readily accessible in case of emergencies. Familiarize yourself with the local veterinary services and emergency pet clinics along your route, just in case your pets require medical attention while on the road.

When it comes to feeding and hydration, maintaining a consistent schedule is key. Ensure that you have an ample supply of your pet's preferred food and fresh water, as well as airtight containers to keep the food fresh. Don't forget to bring along their food and water dishes, as familiar items can provide comfort during the journey. Portable pet water dispensers are also handy for keeping your pets hydrated during pit stops.

In terms of accommodation, many RVs are designed with pet-friendly features in mind. When choosing an RV or planning your trip, consider the comfort and safety of your pets. Look for RVs with non-slip flooring and enough space for your pets to move around comfortably. Create a designated area for them with their bed or blanket, toys, and familiar items to help them feel at home. If you're traveling with cats, ensure they can access a litter box in a secure and easily accessible location.

Another critical aspect of traveling with pets is exercise and playtime. Just like humans, pets need regular breaks to stretch their legs and burn off energy. Plan stops at pet-friendly rest areas, parks, or hiking trails where your pets can explore and get some exercise. Always keep them on a leash and clean up after them to be a responsible pet owner and a considerate traveler.

Weather conditions can vary greatly depending on your RV route, so be prepared to protect your pets from extreme temperatures. In hot weather, ensure they have access to shade and never leave them alone in a parked RV without proper ventilation and cooling. In cold weather, provide adequate insulation and warmth to keep them comfortable. Keep an eye on weather forecasts and adjust your plans accordingly to ensure your pets' safety and well-being.

Finally, consider the entertainment and comfort of your pets during long stretches of travel. Bring along their favorite toys, blankets, or comfort items to help them feel secure and relaxed. Some pets may benefit from soothing music or familiar scents in the RV to reduce anxiety and stress.

In conclusion, traveling with pets in your RV can be a rewarding experience that strengthens your bond and creates lasting memories. However, it requires careful planning and consideration to ensure their safety, comfort, and well-being throughout the journey. By prioritizing safety measures, maintaining a consistent routine, providing proper accommodation, offering exercise and playtime, and protecting your pets from extreme weather conditions, you can enjoy the adventure of RV travel with your furry companions while keeping them happy and healthy on the road.

Pet-friendly national parks and campgrounds

RV camping is a fantastic way to explore the great outdoors while enjoying the comforts of home, and for many RVers, their pets are an integral part of the adventure. Fortunately, numerous pet-friendly national parks and campgrounds across the United States cater to both human and furry family members, ensuring that your RV journey can be enjoyed together with your beloved pets.

Many national parks offer RV camping facilities that welcome pets. One such example is Acadia National Park in Maine. With its breathtaking landscapes, hiking trails, and scenic drives, Acadia is a must-visit destination for nature enthusiasts. The Blackwoods and Seawall campgrounds within the park both accommodate RVs, and pets are allowed in these campgrounds as long as they are kept on a leash.

Yellowstone National Park is another iconic pet-friendly destination in Wyoming, Montana, and Idaho. While there are restrictions on where pets can go within the park, several campgrounds within Yellowstone provide RV facilities and allow pets. The Madison Campground, for instance, permits RV camping and welcomes pets, as long as they are leashed and supervised.

The pet-friendly Joshua Tree National Park in California is a fantastic choice for those exploring the southwestern United States. The Indian Cove and Black Rock campgrounds offer RV camping options, and pets are permitted in these campgrounds, provided they are always on a leash.

In the Pacific Northwest, Olympic National Park in Washington state boasts diverse ecosystems, from temperate rainforests to rugged coastlines. The Kalaloch and Sol Duc Hot Springs campgrounds are pet-friendly RV camping options within the park, allowing visitors to enjoy the stunning scenery with their furry companions.

On the East Coast, the Great Smoky Mountains National Park, which straddles the border of North Carolina and Tennessee, offers pet-friendly RV camping at the Cades Cove and Elkmont campgrounds. While pets are not allowed on most trails in the park, you can still explore the beautiful landscapes from the comfort of your RV.

In addition to national parks, numerous pet-friendly RV campgrounds are scattered across the country. KOA (Kampgrounds of America) is a well-known chain of campgrounds with over 500 locations nationwide, many of which are pet-friendly. They typically offer amenities such as dog parks, pet-walking areas, and even pet-friendly cabins or cottages for rent.

State parks also often provide pet-friendly RV camping options. For instance, California's state parks offer various pet-friendly RV campgrounds, including those in the Redwood National and State Parks and Big Sur State Park.

When planning your RV adventure with pets, it's essential to research and make reservations well in advance, especially during peak seasons. Additionally, be aware of specific pet regulations and leash requirements at each campground or park, and always clean up after your pets to ensure a positive experience for all visitors.

In conclusion, RV camping with pets can be a rewarding and memorable experience. Many national parks and campgrounds across the United States accommodate RVers and their furry companions, allowing you to explore the beauty of nature together. Whether visiting iconic destinations like Acadia or Yellowstone or discovering lesser-known gems, you can enjoy the wonders of the great outdoors with your pets by your side. Just remember to plan ahead, follow park regulations, and make the most of your pet-friendly RV adventure.

Pet safety and etiquette

Traveling in an RV with your furry friends can be a rewarding and memorable experience. However, ensuring the safety and well-being of your pets and being considerate of other campers are essential aspects of pet etiquette when RV camping. By following some key guidelines and being responsible pet owners, you can have an enjoyable and harmonious camping trip while including your pets in the adventure.

First and foremost, ensure that your pets are properly secured while the RV is in motion. Just as you wouldn't travel without a seatbelt, your pets should be restrained for their safety and the safety of everyone on board. Use pet seat belts, harnesses, or carriers designed for travel in RVs to prevent accidents or injuries. Keeping your pets secure also prevents distractions while driving, which can be hazardous.

When selecting an RV campground, research their pet policy and rules. Many campgrounds are pet-friendly but often have specific guidelines regarding leash lengths, designated pet areas, and quiet hours for pets. Always follow these rules to ensure a pleasant experience for both your pets and fellow campers. Be respectful of leash laws, and keep your pets on a leash when outside your RV unless you are in designated off-leash areas.

Responsible waste management is another crucial aspect of pet etiquette. Be sure to clean up after your pets and dispose of their waste in the designated receptacles. Not only is this courteous to other campers, but it also helps maintain a clean and enjoyable environment for everyone. Many campgrounds provide pet waste disposal stations for your convenience.

Consider the comfort and safety of your pets within your RV. Ensure they have access to fresh water, especially during hot weather, and avoid leaving them alone in a parked RV without proper ventilation and temperature control. Familiarize yourself with the campground's pet rules, such as whether pets are allowed in specific facilities or common areas, to avoid any misunderstandings.

It's also important to be mindful of the noise your pets may make. While dogs may bark occasionally, excessive noise can be disruptive to other campers. Try to keep your pets calm and quiet, especially during quiet hours. Be aware of your pet's behavior and promptly address any excessive barking or disruptive actions.

Socializing your pets with other campers and their pets can be a positive experience. However, always ask for permission before allowing your pet to interact with others. Some campers may have allergies, fear of animals, or pets that do not get along well with other animals. Respecting their wishes and boundaries is essential for a peaceful coexistence.

In emergencies, ensure you have your pet's identification, medical records, and necessary medications readily available. Know the location of the nearest veterinary services or emergency pet clinics along your route. It's also a good idea to carry a basic pet first-aid kit in your RV to address minor injuries or health concerns.

In conclusion, RV camping with pets can be a fantastic experience that strengthens your bond and creates lasting memories. However, practicing responsible pet safety and etiquette is essential to ensure a harmonious and enjoyable trip for you and your pets and fellow campers. By following campground rules, securing your pets during travel, cleaning up after them, and being considerate of others, you can enjoy the RV camping adventure with your furry companions while maintaining a positive camping environment.

CHAPTER XII

RVing Etiquette and Conservation

RV campground etiquette

Recreational Vehicle (RV) campgrounds offer a unique opportunity to connect with nature, explore new places, and create lasting memories with friends and family. However, like any communal living space, RV campgrounds come with their own set of rules and guidelines to ensure a harmonious and enjoyable experience for everyone. RV campground etiquette is essential for promoting a sense of community and respect among campers. This section will explore the critical aspects of RV campground etiquette, from reservations and noise control to waste disposal and wildlife interaction.

First and foremost, making reservations and adhering to them is a fundamental aspect of RV campground etiquette. Before heading to a campground, it is crucial to secure a reservation. Campgrounds often have limited space, and arriving without a reservation can lead to overcrowding and disappointment. Furthermore, it is essential to arrive and depart on time, respecting the check-in and check-out times specified by the campground. This ensures a smooth turnover for incoming and outgoing campers, minimizing disruption. One of the most common concerns among campers is noise control. When staying at an RV campground, being mindful of your noise level is essential. Many campers are seeking a peaceful and tranquil environment, so loud music, excessive talking, and other disruptive noises can be a source of frustration for fellow campers. Quiet hours are typically enforced during the evening and early morning to allow everyone to enjoy a peaceful night's sleep. Observing these quiet hours is a basic courtesy that should be noticed.

Another critical aspect of RV campground etiquette is waste disposal. Campgrounds provide designated areas for trash and recycling, which is essential to use properly. Never leave trash outside your RV or scatter it around the campsite; this can attract wildlife and create an unsightly mess. Be sure to follow the campground's rules for waste disposal and recycling, and if you bring a pet, clean up after them promptly to maintain a clean and hygienic environment.

Respecting the natural surroundings and local wildlife is also crucial to RV campground etiquette. Campers should never feed wildlife, as it can disrupt their natural behavior and pose safety risks. Additionally, properly disposing of food scraps and trash can help prevent unwanted animal encounters. If necessary, following campground guidelines for storing food securely in bear-resistant containers is vital to protect both humans and wildlife.

Regarding campfires, campers should be mindful of the rules and regulations in place. Some campgrounds have specific fire size and location rules, while others may prohibit fires altogether during dry or fire-prone seasons. Checking and adhering to these guidelines is essential to prevent accidents and wildfires. Always keep a close eye on your campfire and fully extinguish it before leaving the area.

Furthermore, respecting fellow campers' privacy and personal space is an essential aspect of RV campground etiquette. Campsites are typically designed to provide a degree of separation and privacy, so be mindful of encroaching on your neighbors' space. Avoid cutting through other people's campsites or disturbing their peace and quiet.

In addition to respecting fellow campers, showing respect for campground staff is equally important. Campground hosts and staff work hard to maintain the facilities and provide assistance to campers. Treat them with courtesy and follow their instructions and guidelines. Being polite and cooperative with campground staff can enhance your overall camping experience and contribute to a positive atmosphere within the campground.

Lastly, leaving the campground as you found it is a fundamental principle of RV campground etiquette. Always clean up your campsite before departing, ensuring that it is free of trash, debris, and any damage caused during your stay. Leave no trace of your presence, so future campers can enjoy the same pristine environment.

In conclusion, RV campground etiquette is vital for creating a positive and enjoyable experience for all campers. Reserving your spot, adhering to quiet hours, properly disposing of waste, respecting wildlife, following fire regulations, and showing courtesy to fellow campers and campground staff are all essential components of good campground etiquette. By following these guidelines, you can contribute to a harmonious camping community and make the most of your RV adventures in the great outdoors.

Leave No Trace principles

RV (Recreational Vehicle) travel offers a fantastic way to explore the great outdoors while enjoying the comforts of home on wheels. However, with this convenience comes a responsibility to protect and preserve the natural environments we visit. Leave No Trace principles provide a framework for responsible outdoor recreation, and they are just as relevant for RV trips as for tent camping or backpacking. This section will explore the Leave No Trace principles and how they can be applied to RV travel to minimize our environmental impact.

The first Leave No Trace principle is to plan ahead and prepare. This is especially important for RV trips because it involves more extensive planning due to the size and needs of the vehicle. Proper trip planning includes knowing the regulations and rules of the places you intend to visit, obtaining necessary permits, and researching potential environmental impacts. Knowing campsite availability, waste disposal options, and any fire restrictions that may apply is crucial.

The second principle, travel and camp on durable surfaces, is equally relevant for RV travelers. RVs should stick to established roads, campsites, and parking areas to prevent damage to fragile ecosystems. Avoid off-roading or driving on delicate terrain like wetlands, as the weight and size of RVs can significantly impact the environment.

Managing waste appropriately is the third Leave No Trace principle, and it's especially critical for RV trips. RVs come equipped with bathrooms, kitchens, and waste disposal systems. It's crucial to use designated dump stations for sewage disposal and follow campground rules for trash and recycling. Never dump sewage or greywater on the ground, as it can contaminate water sources and harm the environment.

Minimizing campfire impact is the fourth principle, and while RVs have their cooking facilities, some campers might still use campfires. If allowed by the campground, follow fire regulations, use established fire rings or fire pans, and burn only small sticks and twigs. Extinguish the fire completely before leaving the area, as unattended or improperly extinguished fires can pose a significant fire hazard.

The fifth principle, respecting wildlife, is crucial for all outdoor enthusiasts, including RV travelers. While RVs provide a degree of separation from wildlife encounters, it's still essential to maintain a respectful distance and not feed or approach wild animals. Secure food and trash to prevent attracting wildlife to your campsite, as this can disrupt their natural behavior and create safety risks for both humans and animals.

Leave No Trace's sixth principle, "be considerate of other visitors," is a cornerstone of responsible RV travel. RV campgrounds often bring together diverse people seeking relaxation and enjoyment. To maintain a harmonious environment, keep noise levels down, observe quiet hours, and be mindful of your neighbors. Respect their privacy and personal space, and follow campground rules and etiquette.

Lastly, the seventh principle, "leave what you find," emphasizes the importance of preserving the natural beauty and cultural heritage of the places we visit. Avoid picking plants, disturbing historical or cultural sites, or vandalizing natural features. Leave rocks, flowers, and artifacts as you found them for others to enjoy, and leave behind only footprints.

In conclusion, Leave No Trace principles are not limited to tent camping or backpacking; they are equally relevant and essential for RV travel. Responsible RVers must plan ahead, travel and camp on durable surfaces, manage waste appropriately, minimize campfire impact, respect wildlife, consider fellow visitors, and leave what they find. By following these principles, RV travelers can reduce their impact on the environment, contribute to the preservation of natural spaces, and ensure that future generations can enjoy the beauty of the outdoors as well. RV adventures can be both comfortable and environmentally conscious when Leave No Trace principles are applied with care and diligence.

Supporting the preservation of national parks

National parks are some of the most treasured and breathtaking natural wonders in the United States. From the towering cliffs of Yosemite to the geothermal wonders of Yellowstone, these protected areas offer a glimpse into the country's diverse landscapes and ecosystems. While visiting national parks is a remarkable experience in itself, it's equally important to contribute to their preservation during RV trips. In this section, we will explore how RV travelers can support the conservation and protection of national parks, ensuring these natural treasures remain intact for future generations.

One of the most straightforward ways to support national park preservation during an RV trip is by paying entrance fees and making donations. These fees help fund vital conservation efforts, maintenance of park infrastructure, and educational programs. Most national parks have visitor centers where you can obtain park passes and obtain information about how your contributions are used to protect and enhance the park. By paying your entrance fee and making additional donations, you directly contribute to the well-being of the park you're visiting. Responsible camping is another critical aspect of supporting national park preservation on an RV trip. Many national parks offer designated campgrounds, complete with facilities such as waste disposal stations and fire rings. Camping only in designated areas and adhering to campground rules and regulations is essential. Avoiding off-road camping and staying on established campsite pads minimizes damage to fragile ecosystems and helps protect the park's natural beauty.

Conserving water and energy during your RV trip is a practical way to reduce your environmental impact in national parks. Many parks have limited resources, and conserving water and energy helps minimize the strain on these systems. Simple actions such as taking shorter showers, turning off lights and appliances when not in use, and using energy-efficient appliances can make a significant difference. Additionally, consider using solar panels or generators to power your RV, reducing the need for hookups and conserving energy resources.

Preserving the tranquility of national parks by observing quiet hours and minimizing noise pollution is crucial. These natural spaces are wildlife sanctuaries and provide visitors a peaceful escape. Adhering to quiet hours ensures that both humans and wildlife can enjoy the serenity of these environments. Keep noise levels down, avoid loud music, and be considerate of fellow campers to maintain the peaceful atmosphere that national parks are known for.

Respecting wildlife and their habitats is fundamental to supporting national park preservation. While RVs provide a degree of separation from wildlife encounters, it's essential to maintain a respectful distance and not feed or approach wild animals. Feeding wildlife can disrupt their natural behavior and create safety risks for both humans and animals. Keep food and trash securely stored to prevent attracting wildlife to your campsite.

Proper waste disposal is another essential aspect of preserving national parks on an RV trip. RVs come equipped with bathrooms and kitchens, making it necessary to use designated dump stations for sewage disposal and follow campground rules for trash and recycling. Dumping sewage or greywater on the ground can contaminate water sources and harm the environment. You help protect the fragile ecosystems within national parks by disposing of waste correctly.

Engaging in responsible outdoor activities is also crucial to supporting national park preservation. Stick to established trails when hiking and avoid creating new paths or trampling on sensitive vegetation. Leave no trace by packing out all trash, including microtrash like cigarette butts and food scraps. Abide by fishing and hunting regulations to protect the park's wildlife populations, and follow guidelines for rock climbing and other recreational activities to prevent damage to natural features.

Volunteering your time and expertise can be a fulfilling way to contribute to national park preservation during an RV trip. Many national parks have volunteer programs that allow you to participate in conservation projects, trail maintenance, and educational initiatives. By giving back to the parks you love, you become an active steward of these natural wonders and help ensure their long-term protection.

In conclusion, supporting the preservation of national parks on an RV trip is a responsibility and a privilege. You can play a vital role in safeguarding these remarkable natural treasures by paying entrance fees, practicing responsible camping, conserving resources, respecting wildlife, properly disposing of waste, engaging in responsible outdoor activities, and volunteering your time. National parks offer us a glimpse into the beauty and diversity of the natural world, and we must ensure they remain preserved and pristine for generations to come. RV travelers can make a positive impact by embracing these principles and becoming advocates for conserving our national heritage.

CHAPTER XIII

RV Maintenance and Troubleshooting

Basic RV maintenance tasks

Recreational Vehicles (RVs) provide the opportunity for adventure and travel while bringing the comforts of home on the road. Whether you own a motorhome, camper, or travel trailer, regular maintenance is crucial to ensure your RV remains safe, reliable, and ready for your next journey. This section will explore the essential basic RV maintenance tasks that every RV owner should be familiar with to keep their vehicle in top condition.

One of the first and most critical maintenance tasks is regular inspection of the RV's exterior. This includes checking the roof, siding, windows, and seals for any signs of damage or wear. Look for cracks, leaks, or gaps, allowing water to penetrate the RV. Promptly addressing any issues can prevent more extensive and costly damage down the road. Additionally, inspect and maintain the RV's tires, ensuring they are correctly inflated, have sufficient tread depth, and are free from any signs of damage or dry rot. Proper tire maintenance is crucial for both safety and fuel efficiency.

The RV's engine and drivetrain also require regular attention. Change the engine oil and filter as the manufacturer recommends, typically every 3,000 to 5,000 miles. Keep an eye on other fluids such as transmission fluid, coolant, and brake fluid, and top them off as needed. Regularly inspect the belts and hoses for signs of wear or cracking, as these components are critical for the vehicle's operation. If you are not comfortable performing engine maintenance, consider having a professional mechanic service your RV's engine regularly.

Maintaining the RV's appliances and systems is equally essential for a comfortable and trouble-free journey. Check the propane system for leaks and ensure all connections are secure. Test the RV's electrical system, including outlets, lights, and appliances, to ensure they function correctly. The water system should be flushed regularly to prevent sediment buildup and sanitized periodically to maintain water quality. Regularly clean and inspect the RV's air conditioning and heating systems to ensure they provide efficient and comfortable climate control.

Another crucial aspect of RV maintenance is the care and upkeep of the interior. Clean and inspect the RV's living area, including the kitchen, bathroom, and sleeping quarters, to prevent mold, mildew, and pest infestations. Pay particular attention to seals and seams around windows and doors, as these areas can be vulnerable to water intrusion. Lubricate moving parts, such as door hinges and locks, to keep them in good working condition. RVs often have slide-out rooms or awnings, which require their maintenance. Regularly inspect and lubricate the slide-out mechanisms to ensure they operate smoothly and are watertight when closed. Awnings should be cleaned and checked for tears or damage, and their arms and fabric should be lubricated to prevent rust and ensure easy operation.

Proper waste management is a fundamental aspect of RV maintenance. Empty and clean the holding tanks regularly to prevent odors and ensure the sanitation of your RV's plumbing system. Use the appropriate chemicals and treatments to break down waste and prevent clogs. Ensure that the waste disposal valves are functioning correctly and replace them if they become damaged or leak.

Lastly, don't forget to keep your RV's documentation and records in order. Maintain a log of all maintenance tasks and repairs, including dates, services performed, and any parts or products used. This record can be invaluable for troubleshooting issues and ensuring that all routine maintenance tasks are completed on schedule.

In conclusion, basic RV maintenance is essential for keeping your recreational vehicle safe, reliable, and comfortable for your travels. Regular inspections and upkeep of the exterior, engine, appliances, systems, interior, slide-outs, awnings, waste management, and documentation will help you avoid costly repairs and ensure your RV is ready for your next adventure. Whether you perform these tasks yourself or rely on professional assistance, a well-maintained RV will provide you with years of enjoyable journeys and unforgettable memories on the open road.

Common RV issues and how to address them

Recreational Vehicles (RVs) offer the freedom to travel and explore, bringing the comforts of home on the road. However, like any complex machine, RVs can encounter issues that require attention and maintenance. Identifying and addressing common RV problems is essential to ensure your journey remains smooth and trouble-free.

One common RV issue is battery problems, resulting in dead or drained batteries. To address this, check the battery connections for corrosion and ensure they are tightly secured. If equipped, charge the battery using a suitable charger or the RV's generator. Consider investing in a battery maintenance system to keep your batteries charged and healthy during periods of inactivity.

Leaking roofs are another common concern that can lead to water damage and costly repairs if not addressed promptly. Regularly inspect the roof for cracks, gaps, or damaged seals. Seal gaps or cracks with RV roof sealant, and replace damaged seals as needed. Additionally, check for signs of water damage inside the RV, such as stains or soft spots on the ceiling or walls.

Propane system issues can be hazardous if left unattended. If you smell propane or suspect a leak, immediately turn off the propane supply and ventilate the area. To address this issue, tighten loose connections, check for damaged hoses, and test the system with a propane gas leak detector. It's crucial to have a professional technician address any significant propane system problems.

Inconsistent heating or cooling can be uncomfortable during your travels. Begin by checking the thermostat settings and ensuring they are correct. Clean or replace air filters as needed, as clogged filters can affect the performance of these systems. If the problem persists, a technician may need to inspect the furnace or air conditioner for more complex issues.

Water system leaks can lead to wasted water, damage to the RV's interior, and increased maintenance costs. Inspect all plumbing connections, hoses, and fixtures for signs of leaks. Tighten loose connections and replace damaged parts. If you notice water stains or wet areas inside the RV, trace the source of the leak and address it promptly. Regularly sanitizing and flushing the freshwater system can also help prevent issues.

Many RVs are equipped with slide-out rooms that extend to increase interior space. It can be a significant issue if the slide-out becomes stuck or malfunctions. Check for any obstructions or debris around the slide-out mechanism that may be preventing it from moving smoothly. Lubricate the slide-out rails and gears according to the manufacturer's recommendations. If the problem persists, consult the RV's manual for troubleshooting steps or contact a professional technician.

Tire problems, such as blowouts or flats, can be dangerous and lead to costly damage. To prevent these issues, regularly inspect your RV's tires for signs of wear, cracks, or damage. Ensure they are properly inflated to the recommended pressure and your RV's load is evenly distributed. Carry a spare tire, jack, and necessary tools for roadside tire changes.

Awnings provide shade and protection from the elements, but they can also be a source of problems. Wind, rain, or incorrect operation can damage the awning fabric or arms. To address awning issues, follow the manufacturer's instructions for proper use and care. Repair minor tears or holes in the awning fabric promptly with a patch kit. If the awning's mechanical components are damaged, consult the RV's manual or seek professional assistance.

In conclusion, being prepared to address common RV issues is essential for ensuring a trouble-free and enjoyable journey. Regular inspections, routine maintenance, and following manufacturer guidelines can help prevent many problems from occurring in the first place. For more complex or safety-related issues, it's advisable to consult a professional RV technician who can diagnose and address the problem effectively. By staying proactive and informed, you can continue enjoying the freedom and adventure that RV travel offers while minimizing unexpected setbacks.

Emergency preparedness

Embarking on an RV (Recreational Vehicle) trip is an exciting adventure that allows you to explore new destinations and create lasting memories. However, it's essential to be prepared for unexpected situations that can arise on the road. Emergencies can take many forms, from mechanical breakdowns to medical incidents or natural disasters. To ensure a safe and enjoyable RV journey, it's crucial to have a well-thought-out emergency preparedness plan in place.

First and foremost, having a well-maintained and mechanically sound RV is essential for preventing breakdowns on the road. Regularly servicing your vehicle and keeping up with maintenance tasks can significantly reduce the risk of unexpected engine or system failures. Ensure that tires are properly inflated, brakes are in good condition, and all fluid levels are topped up. Carry a basic toolkit and necessary spare parts specific to your RV model for minor repairs. In the event of a significant mechanical issue, having a roadside assistance plan or an RV-specific insurance policy can be invaluable for getting timely help.

Medical emergencies can happen at any time, so having a well-stocked first-aid kit on board is crucial. The kit should include bandages, antiseptic wipes, adhesive tape, pain relievers, and any necessary prescription medications. Familiarize yourself with basic first-aid procedures and consider taking a first-aid and CPR certification course. Additionally, have a list of emergency contact numbers readily accessible for healthcare providers, local hospitals, and poison control. If you have specific medical conditions or allergies, ensure this information is prominently displayed in your RV, especially if you're traveling with others who may need assistance in an emergency.

Fire safety is a top priority in an RV, where space is limited and fires can spread rapidly. Equip your RV with smoke detectors and carbon monoxide detectors and regularly test their functionality. Carry a fire extinguisher that is appropriate for RV use and know how to use it effectively. Establish and communicate a fire escape plan with your travel companions so that everyone knows how to exit the RV safely in case of a fire. Be cautious when using cooking appliances and heating systems, and always follow manufacturer guidelines for safe operation.

In the event of severe weather or natural disasters, staying informed and having a plan is crucial. Monitor weather forecasts for your travel route and destination, and be prepared to alter your plans if adverse conditions are predicted. Keep a weather radio, smartphone with emergency alert apps, or a NOAA Weather Radio in your RV to receive real-time weather updates. Familiarize yourself with local emergency evacuation routes and shelter locations in the areas you plan to visit. Have a designated safe spot within your RV to take cover during a storm or other emergencies.

Communication is key during emergencies, so ensure you have reliable methods to stay in touch with others. A cell phone with a backup power source or portable charger is essential for maintaining communication. Consider investing in a satellite phone or a two-way radio for areas with poor cell reception. Share your travel itinerary with family or friends and establish check-in times or locations, so someone knows your whereabouts in case you encounter difficulties.

RVs are equipped with electrical and propane systems, which can pose safety risks if not managed properly. Familiarize yourself with the location of electrical and propane shutoff switches and know how to use them in case of a leak or electrical issue. Teach all travelers in your RV how to operate these systems safely to prevent accidents.

Lastly, it's wise to have an emergency kit that includes essentials such as non-perishable food, bottled water, blankets, flashlights, and extra clothing. This kit can be invaluable if you are stranded or waiting for assistance during an emergency situation. Keep important documents, including insurance policies, identification, and vehicle registration, in a waterproof and easily accessible container.

In conclusion, emergency preparedness for an RV trip is crucial to ensure the safety and well-being of all travelers. While RV travel aims to have a relaxing and enjoyable experience, unforeseen emergencies can happen. By maintaining your RV, having a well-equipped first-aid kit, practicing fire safety, monitoring weather conditions, ensuring reliable communication, understanding your RV's electrical and propane systems, and having an emergency kit on hand, you can significantly enhance your readiness to handle unexpected situations. A thoughtful and proactive approach to emergency preparedness will allow you to enjoy your RV journey with peace of mind, knowing that you are equipped to handle whatever challenges arise.

CHAPTER XIV

Capturing the Memories

Photography and journaling tips

Embarking on an RV (Recreational Vehicle) trip offers a unique opportunity to explore stunning landscapes and create lasting memories. To preserve these moments and experiences, photography and journaling can be enriching and enjoyable activities. Capturing the beauty of the places you visit and documenting your adventures allows you to relive your journey and share it with others. This section will explore photography and journaling tips to help you make the most of your RV trip.

Photography is a powerful way to capture the essence of your RV trip. To take memorable photographs, consider the following tips. First, plan your shots by researching the destinations you plan to visit, identifying iconic landmarks, scenic viewpoints, and unique attractions. Having a shot list in mind will help you capture the essence of each place you visit. Second, take advantage of the golden hours, shortly after sunrise and before sunset, when the light is soft, warm, and ideal for photography. Third, experiment with angles and perspectives, trying different approaches to add variety to your photos. Fourth, use the rule of thirds to create balanced and visually appealing compositions. Fifth, focus on details, capturing interesting textures, patterns, and close-ups of flora and fauna. Sixth, don't forget to capture people and moments, as candid shots of your travel companions and shared experiences can be cherished memories.

While photography captures the visual aspects of your journey, journaling adds depth and context to your experiences. Here are some journaling tips to complement your photography. First, choose your preferred medium, whether it's a physical journal, a digital diary, or a combination of both, based on your preferences and goals. Second, establish a routine for journaling, dedicating specific times each day or week to reflect on your experiences. Third, use descriptive language to vividly portray your surroundings, including sights, sounds, smells, and sensations. Fourth, journaling provides an opportunity to process your emotions and thoughts during the trip, so share your excitement, awe, and moments of introspection. Fifth, include practical details like dates, locations, and weather conditions to provide context for your entries. Sixth, tell stories about the people you meet, local cultures, and any interesting encounters or experiences, adding a personal touch to your journal. Seventh, consider attaching mementos such as postcards, ticket stubs, or maps to enhance your written memories. Finally, if you enjoy drawing or sketching, incorporate your artwork into your journal to capture the essence of a place uniquely.

In conclusion, photography and journaling are potent tools for preserving the memories and experiences of your RV trip. Planning your shots, experimenting with angles, and focusing on details in your photography can create a visual narrative of your journey. Complementing your photos with journal entries that describe your surroundings, emotions, and stories adds depth and context to your travel documentation. Together, these practices allow you to capture the essence of your RV adventure and create a lasting record that you, your friends, and your family can cherish for years to come.

Preserving your RV travel memories

Traveling in an RV is an exhilarating and adventurous way to explore the world around us. Whether you're embarking on cross-country road trips or simply enjoying weekend getaways, the memories created during RV travel are often priceless. To ensure that these precious moments are cherished for years to come, it's crucial to have a plan for preserving your RV travel memories. In this section, we'll explore various ways to document and safeguard your experiences, enabling you to relive your adventures and share them with others.

One of the most traditional and timeless methods of preserving RV travel memories is through the art of journaling. Keeping a travel journal allows you to capture the essence of your journey in your own words. You can describe the breathtaking landscapes, the charming towns you visited, and the people you met along the way. A well-kept journal helps you remember the details and lets you reflect on your experiences and personal growth.

In today's digital age, technology offers many options for preserving memories. Taking photos and videos is a common practice during RV trips. Smartphones and digital cameras make it easy to capture the beauty of nature, the excitement of exploration, and the camaraderie of your fellow travelers. Organizing these digital media files into folders or albums can help you quickly access and relive those moments. Don't forget to back up your files regularly to ensure they're safe from unexpected mishaps.

Another way to immortalize your RV adventures is by creating a travel blog or website. Sharing your experiences with others not only preserves your memories but also inspires and informs fellow travelers. You can write about your favorite destinations, RV maintenance tips, and the lessons you've learned on the road. Adding photos and videos to your blog can make it even more engaging. Over time, your blog can become a valuable resource for you and a source of inspiration for others planning their own RV journeys.

Consider turning your travel stories and photographs into physical keepsakes as well. Creating a scrapbook or photo album allows you to showcase your adventures in a tangible way. You can include mementos like postcards, ticket stubs, and maps to add depth to your memories. Scrapbooking can be a creative and therapeutic process that lets you relive your travels while preserving them for future generations.

Don't underestimate the power of souvenirs in preserving RV travel memories. Collecting small mementos from each destination can evoke vivid recollections of your journey. Whether it's a unique trinket, a piece of local artwork, or a simple pebble from a scenic spot, these tangible reminders can transport you back to the time and place you acquired them. Displaying your souvenirs in your RV or home can constantly remind you of your adventures.

In conclusion, RV travel is a remarkable way to explore the world and create unforgettable memories. Preserving these memories is essential to reliving the joy, excitement, and personal growth that come with each journey. Whether through journaling, digital media, travel blogs, physical keepsakes, or souvenirs, there are countless ways to ensure that your RV travel memories endure. By choosing the methods that resonate most with you, you can relish your adventures for years to come and share them with others who seek inspiration and the thrill of the open road.

Sharing your experiences with others

RV travel is not just about the places you go; it's also about the people you meet and the stories you create along the way. One of the most rewarding aspects of RVing is sharing your experiences with others. Whether with friends and family, fellow travelers, or the wider community, sharing your RV adventures can enrich your journey and inspire others to embark on their own. In this section, we will explore the various ways to share your RV experiences and the benefits of doing so.

One of the most immediate and personal ways to share your RV experiences is by inviting friends and family to join you on your trips. RV travel offers a unique bonding experience, allowing you to create lasting memories together. Whether it's a weekend getaway or an extended road trip, sharing the RV lifestyle with loved ones can strengthen relationships and make cherished moments that you'll all treasure. It's an opportunity to introduce others to the joys of exploring the open road and enjoying the freedom of life on wheels.

Social media has become a powerful platform for those who prefer to share their adventures with a broader audience. Posting photos, videos, and updates from your RV travels on platforms like Instagram, Facebook, or YouTube allows you to instantly connect with friends, family, and fellow travelers. Sharing your journey in real-time can create a sense of excitement and anticipation among your followers. It also provides a platform to engage with other RV enthusiasts and exchange tips, recommendations, and stories.

Blogging is another popular way to share your RV experiences more in-depth and reflectively. Maintaining a travel blog allows you to craft detailed narratives of your adventures, share your insights, and provide valuable information to others planning similar trips. Your blog can serve as a resource for fellow travelers, offering advice on destinations, RV maintenance, and the intricacies of life on the road. Over time, it can become a valuable repository of your experiences, inspiring and informing others.

If you are passionate about storytelling, consider writing a book or e-book about your RV adventures. This allows you to delve even deeper into your experiences, providing readers with a comprehensive and immersive account of your journey. Your book can include the destinations you visited, the lessons you learned, the challenges you faced, and the personal growth you experienced. Sharing your story through literature can leave a lasting legacy and inspire others to pursue their RV dreams.

Joining RV clubs and online communities is another way to share your RV experiences while connecting with like-minded individuals. These groups provide a platform to share stories, seek advice, and offer support to fellow RVers. Whether it's a local RV club or an online forum, these communities foster a sense of belonging and camaraderie, allowing you to exchange knowledge and experiences with others who share your passion for RV travel.

In conclusion, sharing your RV experiences with others can be a gratifying aspect of your journey. Whether through personal connections, social media, blogging, writing a book, or joining RV communities, there are numerous ways to share your adventures and inspire others. By opening up about your experiences, you enrich your journey and contribute to a broader community of travelers eager to learn, connect, and explore the world in the unique and adventurous way that RV travel offers.

CHAPTER XV

RVing Community and Resources

Connecting with other RVers

RV travel is a lifestyle that offers unparalleled freedom, adventure, and a sense of community. For those who embark on this journey, one of the most rewarding aspects is the opportunity to connect with fellow RVers. Whether you're a seasoned traveler or just starting your RV adventures, forming bonds with others who share your passion can enhance your experiences in numerous ways. This section will explore the importance of connecting with other RVers and the various avenues through which these connections can be forged.

One of the most common ways to connect with other RVers is by staying at campgrounds and RV parks. These communal spaces serve as hubs for travelers from all walks of life. Campfires, potluck dinners, and friendly conversations with neighbors can quickly turn strangers into friends. The shared experiences of life on the road, from navigating unfamiliar routes to troubleshooting RV issues, create a strong sense of camaraderie among campers. Many RVers find that the connections they make in campgrounds become some of the most cherished friendships of their lives.

In addition to campground interactions, the digital age has opened up new opportunities for RVers to connect. Social media platforms, online forums, and RV-specific apps have become virtual gathering places for the RV community. RVers can share their experiences, seek advice, and exchange information about routes, campgrounds, and travel tips. These online connections provide a valuable support network for those on the road, especially when facing challenges or seeking recommendations from those who have been there before.

Joining RV clubs and organizations is another avenue to connect with like-minded individuals. Numerous clubs are dedicated to RV enthusiasts, each with its own focus and interests, such as vintage RVs, specific RV brands, or RVing with pets. These clubs often organize rallies, events, and gatherings where members can meet in person, share stories, and enjoy the company of fellow RVers who share their interests. Membership in such clubs can provide a sense of belonging and a wealth of resources and expertise.

Attending RV shows and expos is another way to connect with both seasoned RVers and those new to the lifestyle. These events showcase the latest RV models, accessories, and technologies, attracting a diverse crowd of enthusiasts. While exploring the exhibits and attending seminars, attendees can strike up conversations and network with fellow RVers. It's a chance to learn from others' experiences, discover new travel destinations, and make valuable connections within the RV community.

Volunteering while on the road is a unique way to connect with others while giving back to the communities you visit. Many RVers engage in volunteer work, whether it's helping with disaster relief efforts, participating in community service projects, or contributing their skills to local organizations. Volunteering not only creates meaningful connections with local residents but also strengthens the bonds among RVers who share a commitment to making a positive impact during their travels.

In conclusion, connecting with other RVers is a vital and enriching aspect of the RV lifestyle. Whether through campground interactions, online communities, RV clubs, expos, or volunteering, these connections foster a sense of belonging and provide valuable support and camaraderie on the road. Sharing stories, experiences, and knowledge with fellow travelers enhances your journey and contributes to a thriving community of RV enthusiasts united by their love of exploration and adventure on wheels.

Online RV forums and communities

In today's digital age, the internet has become a valuable resource for RV enthusiasts to connect, share experiences, and seek advice. Online RV forums and communities have emerged as vibrant and interactive platforms where RVers can come together to discuss various aspects of their lifestyle. These virtual gathering places play a crucial role in fostering a sense of community, providing valuable information, and creating a support network for those who love the open road. In this section, we will explore the significance of online RV forums and communities and how they enhance the RVing experience.

One of the primary advantages of online RV forums and communities is the opportunity for RVers to share their experiences and knowledge. Whether you're a novice RVer or a seasoned traveler, these platforms provide a space to ask questions, seek advice, and learn from others. From troubleshooting mechanical issues to discovering hidden gems at different destinations, the collective wisdom of the RV community is at your fingertips. This sharing of information not only saves time and money but also promotes safety and confidence on the road.

Additionally, online RV forums and communities serve as a space for camaraderie and connection. RVing can sometimes be a solitary experience, with individuals and families spending extended periods of time on the road. These online platforms offer a sense of belonging, allowing RVers to interact with like-minded individuals who understand the unique challenges and joys of the lifestyle. Friendships often form within these communities, leading to real-world meetups and travel companionships that further enrich the RV journey.

For those planning their RV adventures, online forums and communities are treasure troves of inspiration and recommendations. Members regularly share their travel itineraries, detailing their favorite destinations, campgrounds, and activities. These firsthand accounts offer valuable insights, helping others discover new places and experiences they might not have considered otherwise. As a result, these platforms become invaluable tools for trip planning and creating memorable adventures.

Online RV communities also facilitate discussions on topics beyond travel, such as RV maintenance, upgrades, and modifications. Members can share DIY projects, product reviews, and tips for making life on the road more comfortable and enjoyable. Whether you're looking to enhance your RV's functionality, improve energy efficiency, or simply make it feel more like home, the expertise within these communities can guide you in the right direction.

Furthermore, online RV forums and communities provide a platform for staying informed about industry trends, regulation changes, and RV-related news updates. Members often discuss changes in RV parks, campground reviews, and updates on RV-friendly legislation. Staying connected to these communities can help RVers adapt to evolving circumstances and make informed decisions while on the road.

In conclusion, online RV forums and communities are vital in enhancing the RVing experience. They offer a space for

RVers to share knowledge, connect with others, seek inspiration, and discuss various aspects of the lifestyle. These virtual communities are not just platforms for information exchange; they are places where friendships are formed, experiences are shared, and a sense of belonging is cultivated. For RV enthusiasts, these online forums and communities are invaluable resources that enrich their journey and make the RV lifestyle even more enjoyable and fulfilling.

Recommended books, websites, and apps

Embarking on the journey of RVing is an exciting endeavor that opens up a world of adventure and exploration. Whether you're a newbie looking for guidance or a seasoned RVer seeking to enhance your knowledge and experiences, many resources are available to assist you in your RVing journey. In this section, we will explore recommended books, websites, and apps that cater to RV enthusiasts' diverse needs and interests, offering valuable insights, practical advice, and inspiration.

Books have long been a trusted source of information and inspiration for RVers. "The Complete Idiot's Guide to RVing" by Brent Peterson and April Maher is an excellent starting point for beginners, covering everything from choosing the right RV to campground etiquette and maintenance tips. "RVing Basics" by Bill and Jan Moeller is another comprehensive guide that provides essential information for newcomers to the lifestyle.

For those seeking adventure and inspiration on the road, "Travels with Charley: In Search of America" by John Steinbeck is a classic. Steinbeck's journey across the United States in his camper, accompanied by his faithful dog, Charley, captures the essence of the RV experience and the people and places encountered along the way.

Websites dedicated to RVing are invaluable resources for RV enthusiasts. "RVshare" is an excellent platform for renting or sharing RVs, making it an ideal starting point for those considering RV travel. "RVillage" is a social network specifically designed for RVers, allowing you to connect with other travelers, share experiences, and find local communities and events.

For in-depth information and community support, "iRV2" (International RV Community) is a popular online forum covering a wide range of topics related to RVing. Members can engage in discussions, ask questions, and share their experiences with the community.

Regarding apps, "RV Parky" is a must-have for finding campgrounds, RV parks, and boondocking spots across North America. It provides reviews, amenities, and pricing information, making it easy to plan your stops along the way. "RV Trip Wizard" is an excellent route planning app that helps you optimize your itinerary, taking into account your RV's size and preferences for scenic or efficient routes.

"GasBuddy" is a handy app for locating the best fuel prices, which is especially useful for budget-conscious RVers covering long distances. Additionally, "AllStays Camp & RV" is a comprehensive app that offers an extensive database of campgrounds, rest areas, and other points of interest.

For those interested in RV maintenance and troubleshooting, "RV Maintenance Manual" by Dave Solberg offers a comprehensive guide to RV repairs, maintenance, and upgrades. "RV Mobile Internet Resource Center" is a website and app dedicated to keeping RVers connected on the road, offering information on mobile internet options and equipment.

Whether seeking practical advice, travel inspiration, or tools to enhance your RVing experience, these recommended books, websites, and apps provide a wealth of information and support. The RV community is known for its camaraderie and willingness to share knowledge, making these resources valuable companions on your journey. As you explore the open road and create unforgettable memories, these tools will help you make the most of your RV adventures while ensuring safety, convenience, and enjoyment along the way.

CONCLUSION

"Camp on Wheels: Your Passport to RV Camping in National Parks" is a comprehensive guide that serves as an invaluable resource for anyone seeking adventure, exploration, and unforgettable experiences through RV travel in the United States' national parks. This book opens the door to the world of RVing and provides an extensive roadmap to discover the wonders of America's most cherished natural and cultural treasures.

At the heart of this book lies a passion for adventure and a deep appreciation for the beauty and significance of national parks. It inspires readers to embrace the RV lifestyle and embark on journeys that connect them with nature, history, and the diverse landscapes that define our country. By offering a wealth of knowledge, practical advice, and insider tips, "Camp on Wheels" equips both novices and seasoned RVers with the tools they need to plan, execute, and savor unforgettable trips.

The book's journey begins with a captivating introduction, inviting readers to envision the endless possibilities of RV travel. From there, it delves into the diverse aspects of RVing, covering topics such as choosing the right RV, understanding the essentials of equipment and accessories, mastering maintenance and safety checks, and exploring various factors to consider when selecting an RV. It further enriches the reader's experience with insights into budget considerations, the advantages of new versus used RVs, and packing tips to optimize space and convenience.

One of the book's standout features is its meticulous focus on national parks. It introduces readers to the enchanting world of these protected areas, emphasizing their history, significance, and the myriad experiences they offer. By providing an in-depth look at different types of national park units, the book empowers readers to choose destinations that align with their interests, whether they are passionate about hiking, wildlife, history, or simply seeking solitude in the great outdoors.

"Camp on Wheels" also underscores the importance of thorough research when selecting national parks to visit for an RV trip. It guides readers through the process, from identifying their interests and priorities to consulting official resources, utilizing travel guides and websites, considering logistics, and factoring in budget considerations. The book's comprehensive approach ensures that readers are well-prepared to make informed choices and create personalized itineraries.

As readers progress through the book, they gain essential insights into making campground reservations, navigating seasonal considerations, and understanding the benefits of RV travel. The thorough exploration of these topics enhances the practical aspects of RVing and contributes to a more enjoyable and stress-free journey.

In conclusion, "Camp on Wheels: Your Passport to RV Camping in National Parks" is a remarkable guide that transcends the role of a book and becomes a trusted companion for those who dare to embark on RV adventures. Its wealth of information, vivid descriptions, and expert guidance pave the way for memorable journeys into the heart of America's national parks. By offering a comprehensive understanding of the RV lifestyle and the enchanting world of national parks, this book empowers travelers to experience the freedom, wonder, and natural beauty that await on the open road. Whether you're a first-time RVer or a seasoned enthusiast, "Camp on Wheels" is your ticket to unforgettable adventures, new horizons, and the discovery of a lifetime.

Thank you for buying and reading/ listening to our book. If you found this book useful/ helpful please take a few minutes and leave a review on the platform where you purchased our book. Your feedback matters greatly to us.

www.ingramcontent.com/pod-product-compliance
Lightning Source LLC
Chambersburg PA
CBHW071527150726
48000CB00002B/713